NOT A PODMATCH MEMBER YET?

PodMatch is the premier site for podcast hosts to find interesting and powerful guests.

With two value-packed membership levels, joining PodMatch is one of the smartest and most cost-effective ways to find quality guests for your show.

Joining the PodMatch family is quick and simple. Just visit:

https://podmatch.com/signup/today

PodMatch Host Mastery

A Guide to Finding Interesting Guests and Growing Your Show by Learning From Top PodMatch Host Members

PODCAST HOSTS LOVE PODMATCH!

If you are looking to expedite your podcast booking experience, filling your calendar with high-engagement content while creating value and meaning for your listening community, check out PodMatch and discover your ideal match magic.

—Jeffrey Besecker

My show has a slant towards geography, and I love interviewing people from all over the States, Canada and around the world. PodMatch has opened up opportunities for New Town Big Dreams that simply didn't exist before.

—Luke Menkes

PodMatch is an excellent concept and has helped take the pressure off me wondering what to talk about for episodes and provides listeners with a fresh perspective!

—Danielle McDonald

What you're doing for podcasters like me is so helpful...with the PodMatch platform and the other stuff you're doing, I just want to say thank you for identifying the need and working to solve it.

—Rob Jager

I was able to book enough guests to get my podcast off to a strong start by posting 100 podcasts in 100 days AND publish a digital magazine about the experience, guests, and articles on why people follow podcasts plus more!

—Shannon Peel

I just wanted to say how much I'm loving PodMatch, I only signed up about a week ago and I've already done two awesome interviews and I have more scheduled. Thank you again!

—Natalie Wilkinson

As a busy podcaster, author, and mother of eight, PodMatch has been a huge blessing to me, allowing me to spend less time searching for great guests and more time doing the things I love.

—Liz Meyers

Well done on creating an indispensable resource for the busy podcast host! It's my go-to platform!

—Paul Copcutt

PUBLISHED BY BITE SIZED BOOKS

Copyright © 2022 Bite Sized Books

Printed in the United States of America

Print ISBN: 978-1-7341187-7-3

101722

The publisher gratefully acknowledges the contributing authors who granted permission to reprint the cited material.

This publication is designed to provide accurate and helpful information with regard to the subject matter covered. It is sold with the understanding that the publisher is not engaged in rendering legal, accounting, or other professional advice. If legal advice or other expert assistance is required, the services of a competent professional should be sought. The opinions expressed by the authors in this book are not endorsed by Bite Sized Books and are the sole responsibility of the author rendering the opinion.

Bite Sized Books publishes short, helpful books for business owners, entrepreneurs and corporate leaders who are looking to stand out and differentiate their businesses. Do you have an idea for a bite sized book you would like us to publish? Visit BiteSizedBooks.com for more details.

CONTENTS

PART 3–BONUS RESOURCES

This book is dedicated to all the podcast hosts and guests
who are positively changing the world with their messages.

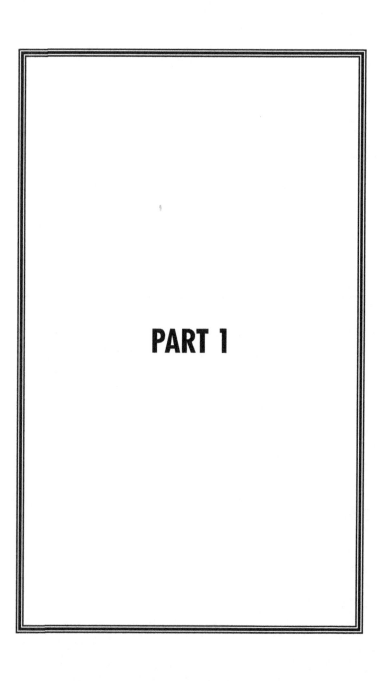

PART 1

WELCOME

ACKNOWLEDGEMENTS

First and foremost, I want to thank the members/ community of PodMatch for giving me the chance to help support them in finding guests for their podcasts. Thank you for trusting me with this critical part of your podcasting process and success!

I want to thank Jesus for giving me the courage to step out of my comfort zone and for the ability to execute this idea. My faith in Jesus is the foundation for the culture we've created within PodMatch!

What we're accomplishing with PodMatch would not be possible without my tech-savvy cofounder, Jesse Hunter. Jesse, you're one of the most brilliant developers I've ever met, an excellent business partner, and the best friend a guy could ever hope to have. You have truly brought PodMatch to life!

I'd like to thank my favorite person, Alecia Sanfilippo. She's incredible when it comes to tackling challenging tasks and supporting members of the community. Without Alecia, I would have never gotten into podcasting in the first place. And without her belief in my ability to lead this business, I would still be in a corporate job. And without her devotion to showing up to serve the PodMatch community every day, you'd all have a lot of questions unanswered! Thank you, Alecia, for being my wife and partner in this journey!

I want to thank each of this book's contributing authors and Mike Capuzzi for putting PodMatch Host Mastery together. Thank you so much for being PodMatch members and being willing to share your best tips and ideas for using PodMatch. I trust readers will learn much from your success, wisdom, and insights!

Lastly, I want to thank you, the reader. If you've picked up this book, that shows me that you will become a valuable member of the PodMatch community. Thank you for investing in yourself! I sincerely hope to get the opportunity to connect with you soon.

—**Alex Sanfilippo**

INTRODUCTION

" **A** lex, I'm having the hardest time finding great guests to be on my podcast." I immediately put another mark on a piece of paper I was holding while responding simultaneously, "I'm sorry to hear that...; I've actually been hearing that a lot today."

A few minutes later, as this struggling podcaster and I wrapped up the conversation, I said to myself, "Man, I really have been hearing this a lot today. I wonder how many times exactly?"

I began counting how many podcast hosts had told me almost the same thing, word for word. I counted, and to my surprise, it was exactly 100! That's 100 podcasters who told me they were struggling to find the ideal guests for their podcasts.

Let me back up. I was collecting this data during March 2020; I was speaking at the Podfest Expo podcasting conference in Orlando, Florida, with nearly two thousand people in attendance. As I exited the stage after speaking, I decided to ask every podcaster I could this question: *"What is your biggest struggle in podcasting right now?"*

The most received answer was the struggle of finding great guests for their shows.

After the event and having these 100 podcasters tell me their struggle, I went home with this newly found/unmet podcasting industry problem. I must admit, after a few days of whiteboarding out some ideas and thinking about the problem, I had come up with nothing close to a solution. I wasn't sure what to do to solve this for the podcasting community. I remember spending time praying and asking Jesus for help/insight.

But then, on March 10th, 2020, it hit me. I was on my back porch doing a workout in the warm Florida sun when a thought crossed my mind that had to be written down.

I quickly ran inside to my wall of whiteboards. The ideas flowed faster than I could write. I have no words to describe it other than it was a divine intervention from God. Here's what I ended up writing down (minus all the technical details):

What if we took what the world of dating apps has done so well, matching people together automatically, and applied that to podcast guests and hosts?

I knew right away that this was the winning idea. I immediately grabbed my phone and called a friend who's a developer. Within an hour of pitching the idea, Jesse Hunter became my cofounder. We had a lawyer draft legal documentation, and each put $2,500.00 into our newly opened business bank account. Then we got to work.

Fast forward to June 15th, 2020, and we launched the beta of PodMatch: "A software that automatically matches ideal podcast guests and hosts for interviews."

Want to know the coolest part? We had 100 people using it during a preview early beta week, the same ones I met at that conference who told me that this was their struggle.

I am thankful to be years into this project now and serving tens of thousands of podcast guests and hosts. Beyond that, and ultimately, I'm even more grateful for the interview podcast episodes that have been released to serve the world of podcast listeners. Together, we're making the world a better place!

Because of PodMatch's exponential growth, we published this compilation book featuring some of the most successful PodMatch members worldwide. We believe this is the best way for current and future members of our growing community to learn from some individuals who have learned to maximize their experience with PodMatch.

As you read, you'll discover that PodMatch Host Mastery includes different perspectives and insights on ways you can use PodMatch to find the most ideal guests for your podcast. This book aims to help you find your flow with PodMatch so you can also become a master of the platform!

Like podcasting, each contributing author has their own way of using PodMatch, and while there will be similarities between how members use the platform, there will also be distinct and valuable differences.

As a result of reading this book, I pray that you find the most ideal guests for your podcast so that you're able to change lives with your content while continuing to grow your influence.

—Alex Sanfilippo

NOT A PODMATCH
MEMBER YET?

PodMatch is the premier site for entrepreneurs, thought leaders and influencers to find some of the world's top podcast shows and be a featured guest.

With two value-packed membership levels, joining PodMatch is one of the smartest and most cost-effective ways to find quality guests.

Joining the PodMatch family is quick and simple. Just visit:

https://podmatch.com/signup/today

PART 2

THE PODCAST HOSTS

Insightful Interviews with Business Owner Authors

Host: Mike Capuzzi

https://podmatch.com/member/mike-capuzzi

Have you thought about writing a nonfiction business book but weren't sure if you could or should? Each week, Amazon #1 best-selling author of *The 100-Page Book* and *The Magic of Short Books*, Mike Capuzzi, interviews published business-owner authors who have written a book to differentiate themselves and create the ultimate competitive advantage.

"The Author Factor Podcast" gives business owners, entrepreneurs and CEOs the book-writing inspiration, encouragement and book-marketing tips they need to write a book that will impact the world and impact their bottom line.

Being a published book author is one of the smartest business decisions you can make. And if you want to hear how others have done it, this podcast is for you!

https://AuthorFactor.com

CHAPTER 1

THE AUTHOR FACTOR PODCAST

Why did you join PodMatch as a Podcast Host member?

I started my interview-style podcast in October 2019, when a friend and successful podcaster helped me change my thinking and focus on the real WHY I should start my own show. I am thankful we had that conversation because being a podcast host has been one of the most rewarding things I have done in business.

My hosting strategy, before joining PodMatch, was inviting business owners I knew (who had written a business-related book). Fortunately, I was able to record the first 62 episodes from my own network when I realized I needed a new way to find great guests. I don't remember exactly how I heard about PodMatch, but I am sure glad I did. Since joining, I've connected with some of the smartest and nicest people, none of which would have happened without PodMatch.

What is one significant way that PodMatch has helped your business/mission?

My show is highly focused. My guests are entrepreneurs, business owners and corporate leaders, and my goal is to inspire them to write their first business-related book or finish the one they started but never completed. I truly have a *Serve the Listener First* mentality and strive to fill each episode with tips, ideas, and encouragement.

In order to do this, I need to bring smart guests on my show, and PodMatch delivers over and over. The level of quality members in PodMatch means I never have to worry about where my next great guest is coming from. This means I can create high-quality content and benefit from the "marketing juice" of producing a weekly show.

What is your daily routine in PodMatch?

I am in PodMatch at least three times per day. Being both a PodMatch Host member and Pod-Match Guest member means every time I am in there, I am looking for two distinct opportunities. As a host, I typically do three things:

1) Review suggested matches and respond.

2) Review requests from PodMatch Guests.

3) Proactively invite guests to be on my show.

What do you recommend as the first thing a new Podcast Host member should do after joining PodMatch?

Read this book ☺, but since you already are, definitely go through the PodMatch Education videos Alex created. Don't just have them playing in the background. Study and apply what he shares starting on day one.

What do you recommend as the second thing a new Podcast Host member should do after joining PodMatch?

Create a powerful and engaging Podcast Page. Study the pages of all the members in this book (see their links in their profiles). Create excellent content for all these parts, including:

• Your Ideal Guest Criteria and Show Tags.

• Your Images.

• Your "Learn More About This Podcast" social media links.

• Your "What You Need to Know + Podcast Flow."

• Your "About the Audience."

Leverage every part of the Podcast Page to your advantage. The time you spend doing this will ensure that PodMatch's algorithm matches you and great guests will find you.

What "beginner's mistake" did you make with PodMatch that you want to warn other members about?

My biggest "newbie" mistake was that I did not create and follow a specific and daily PodMatch Host strategy. Yes, PodMatch is an automated matching system, but your part is not automated. This means that you or someone on your team must be actively going into PodMatch each day (at least 2x) and going through your suggested matches and exploring PodMatch Guests. Pod-Match only works effectively if you do your part every day to use it the way it was designed to be used.

The other mistake I made early on was that I accepted every guest invitation to be on my show. There were a few, in hindsight, who were not ideal for my show. Today, I am more selective in who we "match" and have created a three-step process to ensure quality guests.

What three PodMatch best practices should every Podcast Host use regularly?

1) Use it daily.
2) Tweak your Show Tags to see if you get better matches.
3) Leave positive guest reviews, and request your guests to review your show.

What smart tip can you share for any Podcast Host to use immediately and benefit from?

I mentioned previously that one of the beginner mistakes I made was accepting 100% of the matches that PodMatch generated. It took me a few months, but I finally came up with a simple three-step process to make sure my show is a good match for guests. Feel free to take this idea and customize it for your show. (You can visit the links below and see how I do it.)

When I receive a guest request, I send this message back via PodMatch:

FirstName, thank you for your interest on being on The Author Factor Podcast.

In order to make sure this is a good fit for both of us, I have created a simple, 3-step "VIP guest" process:

Step 1: Review my podcast <u>One Sheet</u>, and review the questions I ask during the interview. Visit https://authorfactor.com/about.

Step 2: Answer this short questionnaire: https://authorfactor.com/questionnaire.

If this looks like it is a good fit for my audience, I will email you Step 3, which is a link to schedule our interview.

Mike

After we receive their questionnaire submission, I review it and respond accordingly. If I feel as if they are an ideal guest, I invite them to Step 3, which is using my online scheduler to schedule our interview.

What additional smart tip can you share for other show hosts to consider using?

I realize I am repeating myself a bit, but I cannot stress how important it is to make sure you bring ideal guests to your show. If you went through the links I shared on the previous page, you will see I've created a "One Sheet" for my podcast. Typically, podcast guests use a One Sheet, but I love the concept so much, I created one for my show.

Not only does it help you clarify your show's message, unique value promise, etc., it also gives potential guests a quick way to understand your show. See mine: https://authorfactor.com/about.

Another smart tip to consider is to create a "preshow" guest funnel and "postshow" guest funnel. Essentially, this means I send reminder emails prior to the interview with all pertinent details. Then after the interview is completed, I send a personal email (using a template I've created) thanking them, letting them know I left them a review on PodMatch and asking them to leave a show review on Apple Podcasts.

What is your final PodMatch "one thing" you want to leave readers with?

Alex and his team have built a Ferrari for matching podcast hosts with guests, automatically. But like any high-performance car, it requires high-quality fuel to run optimally. I believe PodMatch will help you achieve your podcasting goals, if you put the right fuel into it.

What's that fuel?

It's your consistent, intentional, and smart use of it. This is the book I wish I had a year ago. Use it to enable you to attract ideal guests, share your message, impact lives and maximize your PodMatch membership!

Host: Tyler Martin

https://podmatch.com/member/thinkbusiness

Hey Entrepreneurs! Are you going full speed just trying to keep up? Do you feel you have more losses than wins? Join me on a journey as we have real conversations with entrepreneurs about struggles, successes, and tips so we can get you quicker results with no fluff—and get you to your next win now!

http://ThinkBusinessWithTyler.com

CHAPTER 2

THINK BUSINESS WITH TYLER MARTIN

Why did you join PodMatch as a Podcast Host member?

When I started my podcast, I hired a VA (virtual assistant) to find guests. She tried hard, but the guests often weren't a great match for the show. And the process was slow and time consuming. I knew there had to be a better way. So, I searched around and found PodMatch. I was excited to try it to see if I could find guests with less effort and cost.

What is one significant way that PodMatch has helped your business/mission?

On average, I probably get 10–15 guests reaching out each week, and many of those come from PodMatch. The most significant benefit using PodMatch is that the guest profiles are very thorough and have a lot of information and links, so it makes it much easier to determine if a guest is a good match for the show.

What is your daily routine in PodMatch?

My routine is focused on checking messages from guests that have expressed interest in being on the show. From there, I review the profile of the guest and check out their websites and social media profiles. I also will listen to podcasts and videos that they have done to get a feel for their style.

If all lines up, I respond to their message and start the process for scheduling a show.

What do you recommend as the first thing a new Podcast Host member should do after joining PodMatch?

I would say thoroughly complete your profile. Make sure all links work—I am surprised how often people have broken links, sometimes even to their own website.

What do you recommend as the second thing a new Podcast Host member should do after joining PodMatch?

Build credibility in your profile; allow potential guests to see what you are all about. Don't try to be tricky if you don't have any published shows. Just be honest with people. Be responsive and professional.

What "beginner's mistake" did you make with PodMatch that you want to warn other members about?

My biggest mistake was being too scared to require guests with limited info about themselves to set up a planning meeting. I would often book guests I knew little about and often would end up not being a good fit for the guest or the show.

So, don't be afraid to have people set up a short planning meeting. I require it now, and it has helped me tremendously assess the guest fit and prepare for the show.

What three PodMatch best practices should every Podcast Host use regularly?

1) Be clear about who is a good guest for your show, and stick to your criteria.

2) Having said that, don't be afraid to try new things and allow your show to evolve.

3) Learn about the guest, and prepare prior to the show. I find this allows me to navigate through the show and pivot to different topics, which makes for a better show.

What smart tip can you share for any Podcast Host to use immediately and benefit from?

Have fun with the show; do your best to make the guest feel comfortable. Let the guest know you will steer the conversation at times, and let them know that you will raise your hand so they know to let you slide in to the convo and steer the direction.

Every show will be different, but some guests like to get really deep into the details that audiences may find too technical. You need to help the guest move along so they don't spend 10 minutes on a very technical topic that likely won't apply to your audience. I find guests appreciate this direction and help.

What additional smart tip can you share for other show hosts to consider using?

Guests often don't know they are doing it, but some will accidently turn the show into an infomercial.

I will remind the guest to stay away from self-promotion. Let them know that if they deliver good information, their authority and credibility will shine, and people will hunt them down.

True story, I was a guest on a friend's show and knew his show had a very small audience. I didn't expect anything from it. A day after the show published, two people who listened to the show scheduled meetings with me, and one was ready to sign up after a 15-minute conversation. That's the power in a guest podcasting.

What is your final PodMatch "one thing" you want to leave readers with?

Just have fun. Really, that's the biggest thing. Most of us aren't going to be the next Joe Rogan, so just enjoy the ride.

Oh, and one other thing. Just stick with it. I have been publishing weekly now for the last year. My audience growth was slow at first. I often questioned if it was even worth the time and money. Now, my audience is almost doubling every month for the past six months. I am so glad I didn't quit. Plus, it's amazing to meet so many cool and knowledgeable people.

Host: Kevin Kepple
https://podmatch.com/member/kevinkepple

The "Unlock Your Freedom" podcast is a place for leaders to come together for community, inspiration, and the ideas needed to evolve to the highest levels of service and impact.

If you truly want more in your life and business, it's not about doing more, it's about BEING more. This is precisely what the "Unlock Your Freedom" podcast offers you. Join us when you're ready to quantum leap towards your version of success.

https://KevinKepple.us

CHAPTER 3

THE UNLOCK YOUR FREEDOM PODCAST

Why did you join PodMatch as a Podcast Host member?

In 2020, when I launched the "Unlock Your Freedom" podcast, I was focused on interviewing powerful servant leaders with inspired visions for the future. *Sounds great, right?* Initially, I interviewed people from my network, and I quickly discovered that this approach often left me scrambling for guests on a weekly basis. As a business owner, the last thing I need is more work and added stress. Then much to my delight, along came PodMatch to save the day! I've worked with similar sites and companies who offer podcast matching services, but something was always missing. I knew immediately that PodMatch was different. PodMatch offers a cleaner platform with more professional users. Thanks to PodMatch, I've connected with quite a few brilliant and beautiful people. I'm very grateful for this community.

What is one significant way that PodMatch has helped your business/mission?

I love connecting with powerful leaders with servant hearts, and PodMatch makes it easy to know who you are potentially connecting with. Why are servant hearts so important? Mainly because that's the whole point, growth and giving. The more we grow, the more we can give. Being able to find other inspired visionary leaders who willingly share their genius and ideas on how to be more as influencers has helped me and so many of my listeners evolve to higher levels of impact and performance.

Through the various voices highlighted on our show, I am constantly empowered to step into the unknown and innovate in new dynamic ways. In addition, because of PodMatch, I have expanded my network and connected with amazing people that I may never have met otherwise.

What is your daily routine in PodMatch?

Like all things in life, I keep it super simple with PodMatch. Upon logging in, I check the dashboard for to-do's and then go to the messages and respond as necessary. A huge part of the PodMatch genius is in the ease of use. The way to win at PodMatch is to be consistent and show up daily, and respond in a timely manner with grace and respect. I feel it's important to respect all the people who reach out to potentially be a guest on our show. Just because someone may not be a fit for you doesn't mean they don't deserve a respectful response. As with everything, treat people the way you want to be treated.

What do you recommend as the first thing a new Podcast Host member should do after joining PodMatch?

Create a powerful bio that speaks to the audience you're looking to serve. This is the first place people will look when checking out your show. In the bio, you can highlight who you serve, how you do it, and why it matters to you. Be a real person in your messaging and speak directly to who you want to attract. Like attracts like. If you find your show is attracting the wrong people or no people at all maybe, it's a simple messaging tweak that's needed.

What do you recommend as the second thing a new Podcast Host member should do after joining PodMatch?

The second thing you should do is make sure all the other areas of your settings are dialed in, such as your:

- Ideal Guest Criteria and Show Tags.

- Images.
- "Learn More About This Podcast" social media links.
- "What You Need to Know + Podcast Flow."
- "About the Audience."

You don't have to do this more than once if you get it right the first time. The clearer you are here with who and what you are looking for, the easier you will make your life down the road.

What "beginner's mistake" did you make with PodMatch that you want to warn other members about?

One thing that could slow you down, stop you, or stand in the way of success on PodMatch is not having a plan or system for use. *"I'll get to it when I get to it,"* is giving yourself permission to procrastinate and push the things that matter to the side. Have a plan when you log in so that you can be productive versus simply busy while you're there. Be consistent, show up for the people you interact with, and be accountable.

What three PodMatch best practices should every Podcast Host use regularly?

Best practices are treating the other members of PodMatch with respect. Show up regularly with a servant heart. Don't make it all about you because this will only repel the people you truly want. Do what you say you are going to do with love and humility. After you record interviews, mark the interview as complete, and review your guests in your PodMatch account. This is huge because it helps you and your guest gain visibility and offers feedback to both parties.

What smart tip can you share for any Podcast Host to use immediately and benefit from?

Treat people well, and the results will follow. Anytime you connect with someone you resonate with, ask them how you can help them further. Who are they looking to know? Also, don't be afraid to ask your guests who they may know that would be a great guest for your show? People love to help, and you are serving them by having them on your show. So it's okay to ask who they may know. By introducing you to another guest, your current guest gets to help someone they know, so everyone wins.

What additional smart tip can you share for other show hosts to consider using?

"Be the change you want to see." —Ghandi
Always look to serve. Ask your guests, *"How can I help you?"* You have a network, and it will grow using PodMatch. Show up looking to serve your guests and your audience, and don't worry about,

"What's in it for me?" What type of people do you love working with? Be humble, and when you connect with people, be intentional about being kind as opposed to right. Nobody needs another person who is telling them what to do or someone who has all the answers. Be a human filled with love and respect for others. That's the simple plan for a great podcast and an abundant life.

What is your final PodMatch "one thing" you want to leave readers with?

PodMatch is a very cool community full of powerful and wonderful people. You get what you give here, just like everywhere else in life. Show up for the people you have on your show with a servant heart, and good things will follow. Treat people with respect and humility, and you will find many beautiful relationships and ideas. This is a powerful tool, and when used correctly, can be a game-changer for you and your business. Once again, make sure you show up regularly, and be the type of person you love working with. PodMatch works brilliantly because of its members working together to create a community. Your contributions matter, and when you show up and contribute, you add to and create value for everyone.

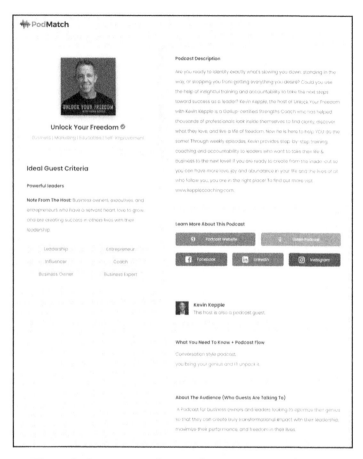

The Unlock Your Freedom Podcast Page on PodMatch

Hosts: Tonya Eberhart & Michael Carr
https://podmatch.com/member/brandfacestar

Tonya & Michael interview serious professionals who share their personal stories and the bold moves that helped them become recognized in their space. They also share personal branding tips and advice for those who want to build a bold, authentic, attraction-based brand that helps them become a sought-after authority.

https://BrandFaceStar.com

CHAPTER 4

BE BOLD BRANDING

Why did you join PodMatch as a Podcast Host member?

Like all hosts, we were seeking guests who would help us to attract an ideal audience and serve that audience with great content at the same time. Unfortunately, we wasted a lot of time and effort in an attempt to find those perfect guests. When we were introduced to PodMatch, it was like podcast heaven and earth met at an awesome intersection.

It allowed us to view guest stories, stats, interviews, and more as well as communicate directly with the people who were seeking to be featured as experts. That made it much easier to attract the right guests and find alignment between our show, our audience, and our goals. Also, we had an opportunity to create a host profile that featured our brand and promoted our show 24/7.

What is one significant way that PodMatch has helped your business/mission?

We've found over 50 guests so far who were not only the right fit, but several of them have also become our clients as a result of that introduction. We've also been able to elevate our presence and gain more authority in the personal branding genre as podcasters. In the beginning, credibility and awareness were the main goals. But now, podcasting has become our most results-driven platform and also a main source of revenue for us. PodMatch helped us achieve all of those goals much faster than we thought possible.

What is your daily routine in PodMatch?

Every morning, one of the first items on our agenda is checking our "matches" section inside the PodMatch dashboard. We message the guests who match our target audience and (kindly) discard the ones that don't seem like a good fit. After that, we check our "messages" section to see who has accepted the match so we can start the booking process. Finally, we head to the "explore" section and tap keywords on the search bar that are aligned to our topics to find new possible podcasts with the same target audience. Once we've finished searching, we check our to-do list and mark the items that have been completed. By following these simple steps, we've matched to successfully book an average of four guests per month.

What do you recommend as the first thing a new Podcast Host member should do after joining PodMatch?

Without question, make sure your personal brand is well defined. You need to be clear about who you serve, how you serve them, what qualifies you to serve them, and how it makes their life better. The top profiles communicate those things effortlessly, and as a result, they attract guests who are a perfect fit for their goals and their audience. Remember that first impressions are often the last impression, so get it right before you put it out there. A well-defined, developed, and displayed personal brand will help you differentiate yourself from other podcast hosts (especially those in your space) and expose the value you bring to the table.

What do you recommend as the second thing a new Podcast Host member should do after joining PodMatch?

Maintain consistency with your brand, your show, and how you use PodMatch as a critical tool in your toolbox. If you don't use it, you lose it. PodMatch is an amazing tool, but it doesn't operate by itself. And although it doesn't take much time, it does require consistent effort in order to be productive and successful. Once your guests have been matched and the interview is successful, make sure to follow up with your guests as well. First, be consistent about leaving every guest a review on PodMatch and on their podcast platform of choice. This practice alone will garner the same number of reviews for you as a host. Additionally, sending something as simple as a personalized thank you card or video goes a long way. Doing these things consistently will bring positive vibes and positive results all the way around.

What "beginner's mistake" did you make with PodMatch that you want to warn other members about?

Don't accept guests based only on what you see in their PodMatch profile. Take the time to review their website links, listen to their podcast (if they have one), and listen to a past interview where they have appeared on someone else's show. We didn't do this early in the process, and we ended up with a handful of guests who could not articulate their brand and position very well or did not have a professional looking background for video (we mainly do video podcasts).

So, do your due diligence and make sure the fit is good with both the subject matter and the way you want your show and guests to appear. Remember, your show is your domain, and you deserve to build it in a way that helps you grow your brand and grow your business.

What three PodMatch best practices should every Podcast Host use regularly?

1) Check your daily matches, and carefully screen them to fit your show criteria.

2) Reply to all of your messages in a timely manner and with kindness.

3) Give back to your guests (a review, thank you card, simple gift, or a referral are the best options).

What smart tip can you share for any Podcast Host to use immediately and benefit from?

Stay focused on the value you deliver to your audience, and don't waiver in that approach. Write down your content criteria, and don't deliver a topic or guest unless it fits your brand and direction. It may be easier to crank out a large volume of shows to fulfill your episode quota, but those shows should meet the "quality" criteria first (rather than just quantity). It is possible to do both with proper brand alignment and planning.

What additional smart tip can you share for other show hosts to consider using?

First, begin your episode with a statement that captures the attention of your audience and promises to deliver a topic they find fascinating. Then, deliver on that promise. Many hosts begin their podcasts with long, drawn out introductions or even ads, and that can cause an immediate tune-out. So, even if your show is the most incredible you've ever done, your audience may never make it past the first 30 seconds. Remember the value you promised because it's a reflection of your brand and the reason your audience is tuning in to your show.

What is your final PodMatch "one thing" you want to leave readers with?

One of the biggest mistakes a podcast host can make is a lack of focus. They cover too many topics and/or attempt to attract "everyone" to listen to their show. This fear of focus is actually one of the top reasons for business failure in any industry. If you're not sure who you serve or what makes you different in your space, stop what you're doing right now and create your own unique brand before you spend one more day or dollar promoting your show. Your life and business will change dramatically as a result.

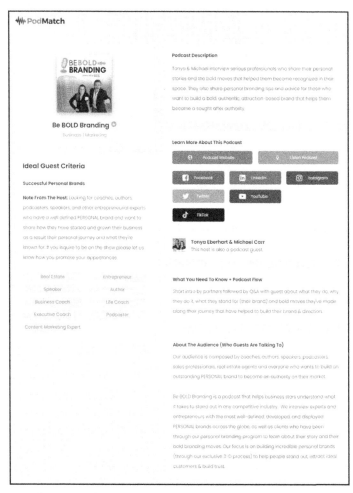

The Be Bold Branding Profile Page on PodMatch

Host: Beate Chelette
https://podmatch.com/member/growtharchitect

Join Beate Chelette, Growth Architect and Business Strategist, as she interviews some of the world's most successful entrepreneurs on her new podcast, "The Business Growth Architect Show."

You'll learn cutting edge business strategies to help you build, grow, and scale your own business through tangible growth strategies you can implement right away in your own business.

Get your favorite note-taking tools ready, listen to the latest episode, and then plan on implementing one stellar growth strategy each week for your own business! Week after week, Beate and her guests will be bringing you tangible strategies you can use to help you grow, build, and scale your business to impact more lives.

You can find more business growth strategies and tools to support you and your business at:

https://BeateChelette.com

CHAPTER 5

THE BUSINESS GROWTH ARCHITECT SHOW

Why did you join PodMatch as a Podcast Host member?

Our brand, The Growth Architect, focuses on strategies that allow our clients to scale their impact and grow their authority. Our clients know where they want to go and have a clear understanding of concepts, like mindset, team building, and leadership. Many have participated in a great deal of personal development and continuous business improvements. Although they have invested in consultants and systems, they are still experiencing business results following the up and down pattern of a sine wave. Most don't have enough hours in their day and know they need a new strategy to grow.

Our clients understand that the next step for growth requires upleveling teams, aligning business units and functions, or elevating the entire company. That is why we constantly look for new strategies to reach them and share with them to help them run their businesses better. We have found that not all strategies work forever, so you always must be on the lookout for where your audience is, what they are interested in, and then find the simplest way to engage with them on that platform.

We had launched an Instagram Instant Authority strategy with one of our partners to reach high-caliber people in our space to be on their podcasts and to build relationships for future collaborations. As we connected with top industry people in our space, like Greg Reid, Brad Sugars, Mark Joyner, and Peter Sage, we started to interview them. But at that caliber, you can't make a promise that you do not keep. That meant that we had to start a podcast to publish these interviews. That's how "The Business Growth Architect Show" was launched.

Because we already had podcast guesting as one of our strategies in place last year, we were familiar with what PodMatch offers. We loved the platform for guesting, so it was a natural, easy decision to use it for hosting. PodMatch makes finding guests, vetting them, signing releases, and communicating very easy.

What is one significant way that PodMatch has helped your business/mission?

PodMatch is the reason we have launched a podcast host mastermind. We designed strategies, our own workflows and blueprints, and a monetization piece around hosting our own podcast. We had many other hosts reach out wanting to know how we turned one podcast episode into 15–25 content pieces and how we booked all those high-caliber guests even though we had just started.

Many podcast hosts think the money is in waiting until they get downloads so that they can get sponsors, and that is where the money is. But we found that this is just one piece and only available for a small percentage of hosts and very rarely the case for business owners who host a podcast to increase their reach. The strategy is just different. That's why we added a monetization piece that podcasters can start immediately. We are calling this *Growth Authority: Grow Your Podcast into an Authority Building Machine and Monetize Your Expertise*. It is for podcasters who want to maximize their content reach with proven turn-key strategies that generate qualified leads, grow your authority as an industry leader and monetize your experience through your podcast.

What is your daily routine in PodMatch?

We designed an entire workflow around Pod-Match. My VA team is in PodMatch daily; they know our criteria for guests and the industries we are interested in. Because our podcast is about business strategy, we eliminate guests in specific categories, like personal fitness, travel, or nutrition. PodMatch allows us to vet from within the program very quickly. If it looks like a good fit, we schedule 15-minute conversations. We follow up in PodMatch with the scheduling as well. The pass button keeps things easy if it is not a good match.

What do you recommend as the first thing a new Podcast Host member should do after joining PodMatch?

I learned this from Chris Williams from Group Coach Nation. Write your profile like a sales page, and make sure you tie what your business sells into your profile. Since I've done that, I have noticed the difference. There are so many Pod-Match profiles where the guest and the host focus on all the things they can discuss. That is not a good strategy. You only want to talk about topics on your podcast that directly tie in with what you do because the ultimate goal is to make sales, not just to be liked. Even if you think that podcast hosting is about downloads and likes and shares, you are a business, and you need to think revenue.

What do you recommend as the second thing a new Podcast Host member should do after joining PodMatch?

You must have a strategy for whom you want on your podcast. As I already outlined, there are things we just don't want to talk about because it is irrelevant to our niche. Resist the temptation to think that just because someone is "nice" or looks "interesting" or has their sales pitch down that it translates into them being a good guest. Make sure your guests:

1) Elevate you and your expert status.

2) Get notoriety for your podcast.

3) Help you grow your business.

What "beginner's mistake" did you make with PodMatch that you want to warn other members about?

Many people look great on paper, but they sound incoherent, have low energy, are plain boring, or don't take it seriously. When you get a DM on PodMatch that asks you what topic YOU would like THEM to talk about—RUN. It means they don't know their business well enough to bring focus to the interview and are the most likely to ramble through different topics making the interview unusable. Everything you do is focused and deliberate and must follow a strategy. I hope I drive this point home.

What three PodMatch best practices should every Podcast Host use regularly?

1) Follow up, follow up, and follow up. Once the interview is done, that is when the real work begins. You schedule a call to see where the business opportunities are.

2) Thank your guest.

3) Create good swipe copy, graphics, and audiograms, and make sure you notify your guests when the interview goes live so they can cross-promote.

What smart tip can you share for any Podcast Host to use immediately and benefit from?

Make sure you have a Podcast Host strategy in place. It includes an avatar of your ideal guest and a clear direction of what your podcast is about. Say no when it doesn't feel right. Guard your time to spend it with those guests who will drive your business forward. In so many words: Your podcast is one of your business strategies; please treat it as such.

What additional smart tip can you share for other show hosts to consider using?

Please invest in the Professional version of Pod-Match. You get out of it what you put in it. If you are looking for a deal or bonus, you will also attract people who want a deal or a bonus from you.

What is your final PodMatch "one thing" you want to leave readers with?

I am in this book because I had Mike Capuzzi on my podcast. I love his idea about a shook™ (short, helpful book), and we are working on an additional collaboration outside this one. Because I am launching a strategic Podcaster Mastermind, I am in touch with Alex Sanfilippo, one of the creators of PodMatch. Remember, you are building relationships; treasure them. People either become your fans, are indifferent, or they don't ever want to talk to you again. An army of ambassadors with great things to say about you is an excellent business investment.

The
SMALL
BUSINESS
STORYTELLERS
WITH SETH SILVERS

Host: Seth Silvers

https://podmatch.com/member/sethsilvers

O n "The Small Business Storytellers with Seth
Silvers" podcast, Seth shares some of the most
unique business stories you have never heard. Join
Seth as he dives into what the key factors are for
businesses making a purposeful impact in their
industries, and learn how to apply those lessons to your
own business.

https://SuccessWithStories.com

CHAPTER 6

THE SMALL BUSINESS STORYTELLERS

Why did you join PodMatch as a Podcast Host member?

Finding good guests for a podcast can be challenging. You may have a great show concept and even know what kind of guests you want to have on, but how do you find them? I was thrilled to join PodMatch because it helped me filter through people that wanted to be a guest on "The Small Business Storytellers." A huge contributing factor to someone being a great guest is whether or not they want it. PodMatch members want to be there, which means they are usually high-quality guests.

What is one significant way that PodMatch has helped your business/mission?

PodMatch has helped our business by filling our podcast with guests that care about delivering value for the audience rather than just wanting it to be on a show where they can deliver a sales pitch for themselves. This has helped our network expand as we build relationships with the guests that are on our podcast.

What is your daily routine in PodMatch?

Every week, we log in to PodMatch to see the messages and requests that we have. It is incredible to have a specific inbox and dashboard specifically for our potential guests. When we access PodMatch, we are looking at the profiles of those who submitted as well as their messages. When we do that, we look to see if the guest has researched our show and can add value or if it seems like they are just wanting to pitch their own business.

What do you recommend as the first thing a new Podcast Host member should do after joining PodMatch?

Explore the site. Look at other shows' profiles and take note of what you like and what you don't, in regard to how they talk about their show. It is important for you to not only see what things other shows are doing that don't align with your style or vision but also see how other shows are talking about themselves that will add value to your profile as well.

What do you recommend as the second thing a new Podcast Host member should do after joining PodMatch?

Take the time to build out your profile well, and be thoughtful about your keywords and descriptions. When we did this, we had almost 50 qualified requests within a few hours.

What "beginner's mistake" did you make with PodMatch that you want to warn other members about?

Our first mistake was accepting everyone who requested. I thought because it is a filtered platform that everyone was a good fit. You are the host and the leader of your show, therefore, you have a responsibility to still do homework to ensure the guest is a good fit. If they aren't, that is on you.

What three PodMatch best practices should every Podcast Host use regularly?

First, and this is not unique to PodMatch, but you need to be diligent about communicating with your guests. If you fall behind in your communication, that's a reflection on your brand and the relationships with your guests. It makes it seem like you just want another episode done, as opposed to learning from their experience and sharing it with your audience.

The second recommendation is to be crystal clear on what type of guests you want and who your content is for. If your content is for everybody, it is likely impacting nobody.

The third recommendation is to be a great host. That may sound simple but the majority of podcast hosts out there aren't doing all they can to be a great host. Research your guest, plan out questions, get yourself in the right mindset, and perform the interview with your guest in mind.

When you do this, you will not just see your show grow because your interviews are serving your audience better, but you will see your reputation on PodMatch increase as well. You will be rated as a stellar host and others will want to be on your show.

What smart tip can you share for any Podcast Host to use immediately and benefit from?

Listen to your most recent episode and ask yourself if the episode got you excited. If you are not excited by your content, you need to change your content. When you love your content and are excited to show up, that will show in your content. There are so many podcasts out there, and you creating content just for the sake of having more content doesn't benefit anyone. Make sure you love your show.

What additional smart tip can you share for other show hosts to consider using?

Don't worry about how famous the guest is as much as you worry about the content being great. Historically, on my show and my client's shows, the most downloaded and shared episodes are the ones with relatively unknown guests who deliver insane amounts of value. You want to create content and have guests that can deliver value, and when you do that, your audience will share the episode. Nobody wants to share another episode with a celebrity talking about surface level topics.

What is your final PodMatch "one thing" you want to leave readers with?

Don't quit. PodMatch is an amazing tool that helps make our journey as podcast hosts easier and more sustainable, but I encourage you to continue to iterate your show, listen to your audience, and create content you love. When you do this over time, it will build a brand for you that you love and that your audience loves sharing with their community.

Host: Jonathan McLernon

https://podmatch.com/member/jonathanmclernon

This podcast is host Jonathan McLernon's passion project! As human beings, we are wired to learn from stories, especially real-life stories that we can relate to. This show is about sharing people's stories of overcoming significant obstacles and adversity in their life. The show can be gritty and vulnerable, but it is also hopeful, inspiring and entertaining.

It's an opportunity to explore the stories that take place between the "before" and "after" photos—the powerful experiences that shape who we become. We dig into the obstacles we overcome and HOW we overcome them. And ultimately, we want to shine a light on our powerful human potential and the possibilities that lie within us.

https://FreedomNutritionCoach.com

https://JonMcLernon.com

CHAPTER 7

BETWEEN THE BEFORE & AFTER

Why did you join PodMatch as a Podcast Host member?

I had originally put my podcast on other podcast booking sites before learning about PodMatch, and I was being inundated with poor-quality guest requests that were not at all suited for my podcast but rather just guests copying and pasting messages to try and get booked on as many podcasts as possible.

When I learned about PodMatch, and how they matched guests and hosts, I was immediately hooked in. The number of guest requests that have come in have dramatically lessened, which is a great thing, because I have a limited number of spots available. But more importantly, the QUALITY of the guest requests has significantly increased, saving me a LOT of time in the process while helping me to improve the quality of my show.

What is one significant way that PodMatch has helped your business/mission?

PodMatch has ensured that I can screen guests more effectively. Higher quality, more targeted guests means that I produce higher quality content, which in turn means that my show grows. The efficiency with which I can do this means that I can use those time savings to produce more episodes. It ends up being a virtuous cycle that ultimately means my show will be able to keep moving forward for years to come.

What is your daily routine in PodMatch?

I log in usually once a day, sometimes more if I'm getting a lot of incoming messages. I check my dashboard, see what tasks are on my To Do list, and take care of the high-priority ones.

I make a point of replying to every single guest request even if I feel that they aren't a good match for my show because I appreciate that people have taken time out of their day to send a request my way, and extending them the courtesy may mean that down the road, if our paths cross, they might remember that I didn't just brush them off.

I'll then pop over to the Explore section to see what new and featured guests show up and see if any have intriguing stories that might fit my podcast. If I find a good match, I'll reach out and invite them to be on my show.

What do you recommend as the first thing a new Podcast Host member should do after joining PodMatch?

I'd say to go through the PodMatch education videos. They're short, to the point, and they very quickly bring you up to speed on all of the powerful features that PodMatch has built into the software. Alex and his team have built a powerful and efficient software that will save you a ton of time, so knowing how to make the most of this powerful platform means that you will be able get a massive amount of value from it.

What do you recommend as the second thing a new Podcast Host member should do after joining PodMatch?

Play around and explore and get a feel for the platform. Check out other host profiles, and check out guest profiles, and just get comfortable. Don't worry about getting your profile perfect the first time around. If you're in the podcast game for the long haul, your show will likely grow and evolve. But have a look at the profiles of people on the Top 10 leaderboard, and you just might find a great fit for your show on your first day on the platform.

What "beginner's mistake" did you make with PodMatch that you want to warn other members about?

I think "warn" is a strong word, for such a user-friendly and powerful software, but I'd say my biggest mistake (that I'd like to alert people to) was feeling the pressure to accept a lot of the guest requests that came rolling in early on. I felt bad about saying no to people who had taken the time to write a sincere message. And I felt that as a newer user, I didn't want to come across as a snob.

What made this easier as time went on was taking the time to write a short (but sincere) reply even if I felt they weren't a good fit. I recommend always taking a few minutes to check out their profile and really determine whether they would be a good fit for your show.

What three PodMatch best practices should every Podcast Host use regularly?

I'd say use the search filters on the Explore page. The filters can be quite detailed and powerful and really lead to finding some amazing guests that might take a while to come up via your matches. You know your show even better than the PodMatch algorithm (though it does a pretty amazing job of finding matches).

Don't be afraid to punch above your weight when looking for guests on your show, but be reasonable in your expectations. There are guests with large online followings, which might be a good fit for your show, but they might also get a lot of requests to appear on shows. So don't be put out if you don't get a reply or an acceptance of your invitation.

When sending an invitation, be concise and to the point. Allow your profile to carry the weight of your show details. Your guests may be very busy, so include these key elements in your invitation:

1) A quick one-sentence synopsis of your show.
2) The reason(s) why you feel that they would be a good fit to be a guest on your show.
3) The benefit(s) they would receive from appearing on your show, i.e., what's in it for them.

What smart tip can you share for any Podcast Host to use immediately and benefit from?

I'm very much a fan of efficiency because I feel that one of the reasons that podcasts fail to continue is the potential time investment in creating and publishing a podcast. I recommend having a guest request questionnaire. And with the right questions, you can have your guest write the majority of your show notes for you.

For example, in my guest request form, I ask my guests to write a short four-to-five sentence bio in the third person. It's important to not make this questionnaire too onerous overall, but it can make life easier. I may still take a quick look and slightly edit, but having a guest fill in the questionnaire has saved me a lot of time when it comes to preparing and publishing my episodes.

What additional smart tip can you share for other show hosts to consider using?

This tip won't be for everybody, but I would suggest that you consider live-streaming your podcast on social media, if you run a "no-edit" style podcast, to increase awareness and viewership of your show.

Video viewership of podcasts is growing significantly more popular, so it makes sense to take advantage of this trend. There are several different software programs out there that do this, and I would suggest trialing more than one before settling on which one is the best fit for your show.

What is your final PodMatch "one thing" you want to leave readers with?

Podcasting is a different beast than social media, and the metrics look totally different. And if you go into podcasting with misplaced expectations early on, you may find yourself getting discouraged. The podcasts that succeed in the long term are the podcasts that stay in the game.

There are so many different ways to utilize podcasting to support your business and mission that go beyond the typical "vanity metrics." Podcasting can give you the ability to network and connect with a tremendous variety of inspiring and amazing individuals, and it opens so many doors.

PodMatch has made it their mission to support podcasters in as many ways as possible to ensure that they are able to continue to podcast, through steps, such as revenue sharing, podcast awards (plaques), the "Best of" podcast websites, and as such, they are head and shoulders above any other podcast-booking service.

Take full advantage of the support, events and community that Alex and his team have put together so that you will be able to continue to podcast for years to come.

Host: Wade Galt
https://podmatch.com/member/wadegalt

Have you ever had a 3-day weekend and thought, "Wow, I'd like to do this all the time!"? If so, this is for you. I help entrepreneurs and business owners impact more people and make more money in less time, doing what they do best so they can enjoy their family, friends, freedom, and lives outside of work.

We discuss making time for family, personal finance, budgeting, freelancing, recruiting, creating awesome vacations, your bucket list, leveraging technology, automation, 80/20 investing, social media, avoiding common $10,000+ mistakes, time optimization, productivity, delegation, sales, cost-effective marketing & outsourcing, networking, how to get there step by step, and a lot more.

Regardless of where you are in your journey, this podcast will help you get started.

https://www.3DayWeekendEntrepreneur.com

CHAPTER 8

THE 3-DAY WEEKEND ENTREPRENEUR

Why did you join PodMatch as a Podcast Host member?

I joined PodMatch to attract win-win "GIVER" guests who could serve my audience and possibly become live event presenters and promotional partners.

Your guests owe you nothing, but wouldn't it be cool if they treated you like a partner rather than a place to dump their content, leverage your audience, and run? If you set up your guest filters and use PodMatch in a specific way, you can make this very likely to happen.

Producing a high-quality podcast and related social media assets requires an investment of hours of your time and/or hundreds of dollars per episode or more.

Your guest-filtering process can either attract podcast guests looking to leverage your time and effort without considering how they serve you and your business model or you can find people who look out for your best interest and theirs.

What is one significant way that PodMatch has helped your business/mission?

PodMatch helps me quickly identify, filter, and attract high-quality "GIVER" guests. (Many have presented at my live events, and some have become promotional partners.)

To create win-win relationships, it's important to explore the patterns and profiles in PodMatch of people who are primarily givers versus takers.

When you work with takers, you're much more likely to get a lower ROI on your podcast and related product sales, feel taken advantage of, and be more likely to podfade or quit.

When you work with givers, you're more likely to be inspired by your podcast and guests, happily do the work even if your podcast is not immediately profitable, and create greater opportunities for partnerships and long-term income.

Podcasting is a long-game strategy. If you hate the process and dislike your guests or resent them, you'll be much more likely to fade or quit.

What is your daily routine in PodMatch?

I check PodMatch weekly (with virtual assistant help) to screen and identify ideal guests. The VA uses a screening criteria checklist I created to filter applicants. I review the ones she believes will be good guests, do my own review, then reach out to the guests I hope to interview.

What do you recommend as the first thing a new Podcast Host member should do after joining PodMatch?

Make your profile crystal clear about EXACTLY who you are looking for, and mention who you're NOT looking for on your show (and share a polite reason why).

What do you recommend as the second thing a new Podcast Host member should do after joining PodMatch?

Create a list of red flag phrases, trends, or patterns you see from people who are not great guests so you can create a standard operating procedure and eventually delegate most of your guest screening to a virtual assistant.

- The VA I work with shares their recommendations and does about 80% of the screening work.

- I quickly review the NOs, but since they are based on my criteria, they're almost always accurate.

- I make the final decision to invite a guest.

LOOK FOR AND CHOOSE GIVERS AS GUESTS

Choose people who:

1) You are interested in for their work.

2) Are great for your audience.

3) Are great for your business.

Don't leave any one of these out.

You invest too much time, money, and effort to have someone simply use your platform to further their work without supporting your work as best as they can.

Any person who won't share and/or comment on your episode clips of their interview (if produced in a high-quality manner) is not a good guest for your show OR your business.

Choose guests who will (1) share your work, (2) host you on their show, and (3) be future promotional partners.

CHOOSE GUESTS FOR YOUR SHOW LIKE YOU'D CHOOSE A WORK OR LIFE PARTNER.

BE PICKY!

Every time you have a mediocre guest on your show, you waste the time and money you invested in producing that episode AND you weaken your reputation a bit.

What "beginner's mistake" did you make with PodMatch that you want to warn other members about?

Initially, I accepted podcast guests that were competent but not a great match for my podcast message or audience. Usually, these guests did little to share the social media assets I created or the episode because there was weak synergy between their message and my audience.

What three PodMatch best practices should every Podcast Host use regularly?

1) Reply to every person who applies to your podcast as a guest whether you are accepting them or not.

2) Use template messages when replying to guests, but customize the first part.

3) Offer "thank you for applying" gifts to people you decline as guests (even if it's your freebie).

What smart tip can you share for any Podcast Host to use immediately and benefit from?

Creating shareable video clips for LinkedIn, Facebook, TikTok, Instagram Reels, and YouTube Shorts is one of the best ways to maximize podcast episode exposure and get guests excited to share your posts and attract new listeners plus ideal guests. (Use for solo episodes, too.)

What additional smart tip can you share for other show hosts to consider using?

Focus on the message and content above perfecting audio quality. Many of us grew up hearing motivational cassette tapes with subpar audio quality, yet we listened repeatedly because of the message.

Great content with mediocre audio will consistently outperform mediocre content with perfect audio.

What is your final PodMatch "one thing" you want to leave readers with?

Decide what you most want out of your podcast!

Notice the difference between your interviews with TAKERS vs. GIVERS. For each, consider...

- *How well or poorly did things flow?*
- *How well did they support the episode?*
- *Are you still in contact with them?*
- *Would you do it again?*

You can have amazing guests who don't partner with you or amazing guests who partner with you. The second situation is far more enjoyable, fulfilling, and profitable.

Choose great people to share your journey!

TAKERS VS. GIVERS (In PodMatch)

PODMATCH	GIVERS	TAKERS
Pitch	Usually do their own pitches (or a Virtual Assistant screens, and guest reaches out)	Often mass message from a VA with hyped up language but no signs of familiarity with your show
Pitch Message	Custom message	Mass message
Pitch Focus	Your audience	Them
Popular Pitch Pronouns	"You"	"I"
Pitch Reason	Specific reasons why they like your show & want to be on it	Weak or self-centered reason
Pitch "I love your show"	Specific reference to episode contact and why they like it	Generic hyped compliments (i.e., "Amazing Show!") with reference only to episode or podcast title (not content). Like a bad pick-up line.
Pitch (Authors)	Authors offer to send you their book in their pitch.	Author wants book reviews and for you to buy book.
Pitch Vibe	Low pressure, hopeful, polite	High pressured, entitled, often condescending (long list bragging about them and how you'd be lucky to have them)
Bio	About them and how they their work impacts others.	Primarily about them
Pre-Interview	Will do a pre-interview to make the episode customized and great for your audience. (This can be 15 minutes before interview to be time efficient).	Won't do them for any reason
CTA	Freebie or gift	Sales page
Best Episode	Episodes on other shows	Solo Episodes Only

Host: Claudia Garbutt

https://podmatch.com/member/claudiagarbutt

Do you want to build a million-dollar business without sacrificing your health, relationships, or happiness? Welcome to the "Wired for Success Podcast," the show for ambitious, mission-driven entrepreneurs who want sustainable success on all levels!

As a molecular biologist turned mindset & high-performance coach for high-achievers, I share my own experiences and interview leading scientists, industry experts, and successful entrepreneurs to teach you how to stay happy, healthy, and productive while building your legacy.

I also feature the best nonfiction books from the science, self-development, and entrepreneurship categories in the "Leaders Are Readers Wired for Success Book" segment of my show.

https://WiredForSuccess.solutions

CHAPTER 9

WIRED FOR SUCCESS PODCAST

Why did you join PodMatch as a Podcast Host member?

I remember getting an email telling me about this new platform that matched podcast hosts with podcast guests. Normally, I definitely don't check out every cold email about a new product or service, but this sounded like a really helpful tool.

I'm fortunate and grateful that finding amazing podcast guests has never been a problem for me. I actually had a waitlist of 50–60 potential guests even before I launched my show. And when I launched my podcast straight into the Top 10 charts, my waitlist quickly grew even longer. Figuring out whom to invite to the show was quite time-consuming though because I want to make sure that each episode delivers great value and that I invite guests who can share inspirational stories, profound insights, and practical information with my listeners.

If only there was a way to quickly screen a potential guest's bio, achievements, credentials, etc., without having to search for their website and/or stalk them on social media... Alex must have read my mind when he created PodMatch! Thank you, Alex!

What is one significant way that PodMatch has helped your business/mission?

My show is all about helping ambitious, mission-driven entrepreneurs build million-dollar businesses without sacrificing their health, relationships, or happiness.

To do that, I interview scientists, thought leaders, industry experts, and super-successful entrepreneurs to discuss their research findings or the frameworks, mindsets, and high-performance habits that allowed them to build sustainable success.

Because I want my guests to learn from the best in their respective fields, I need a screening tool or process to validate potential guests.

PodMatch provided a great solution to this screening problem as I can quickly look at someone's profile to see if they are a good fit for the show or not.

Believe me, if you host your own high-quality podcast, you'll get a lot of guest requests. And as I tell aspiring podcasters whom I help to launch their own authority marketing podcast: It's YOUR responsibility as the show host to make sure you vet potential guests and only invite those who are a good fit for your show and audience.

What is your daily routine in PodMatch?

Ok, this is awkward. But I'll be honest: I do NOT have a daily PodMatch routine. I used to log into PodMatch daily or at least two to three times per week, to review new matches, reach out to potential guests, and answer messages. But with my waitlist being super long, I stopped doing that because I simply didn't need more guest recommendations. I now usually log in on Mondays and Fridays to answer messages and connect with potential new guests.

What do you recommend as the first thing a new Podcast Host member should do after joining PodMatch?

Create a great show profile that attracts the RIGHT guests. This is so important! You will always have people who reach out even though they are NOT a good fit for your show. But you can drastically reduce that number by creating a strong show profile that ATTRACTS potential guests who are a good fit and REPELS those who are not. This is what you want. You don't win an award for getting the most guest requests. You don't want to waste your time having to go through a ton of messages from people who are NOT a good fit.

Therefore, you want to be very clear and specific about what you and your show stand for. This is NOT just about using the right keywords to feed the algorithm though. Keep in mind that there are also real humans who proactively look for the right shows to be on and agencies who are looking for the perfect shows for their clients. So yes, include keywords, but don't stuff your show description with lots and lots of them trying to please the algorithm. Your show profile needs to be attractive to your ideal GUEST.

What do you recommend as the second thing a new Podcast Host member should do after joining PodMatch?

Apply what you're learning in this book from people who have been using PodMatch successfully so that you don't waste your time trying to figure this out on your own. Also, get your information straight from the source by watching Alex's introduction videos that explain PodMatch's best practices and how it works.

What "beginner's mistake" did you make with PodMatch that you want to warn other members about?

The focus of your show may shift as it evolves, or you may add something to your show concept, and that's totally fine. Just make sure you update your profile after those changes.

For example, I recently started a new book club segment on the show that features the best non-fiction books from the science, self-development and entrepreneurship categories, but I never updated my show description and tags to reflect that change. I just did this today and had another five new guest requests within two hours.

What three PodMatch best practices should every Podcast Host use regularly?

1) Make sure your show profile is up-to-date and attracts the RIGHT people for your show and audience.

2) Answer your messages and always be kind, respectful and appreciative in your conversations.

3) Leave guest reviews, and ask guests to review your show too. This is a great way to show your appreciation and build social proof.

What smart tip can you share for any Podcast Host to use immediately and benefit from?

If you sign up to PodMatch as a hybrid member (meaning you're a guest AND a host), you'll probably find that your host profile will attract a lot more interest and messages.

In my experience, if your show profile is done well, you don't have to do much to attract a lot of potential guests. If you want to get booked as a guest on other podcasts though, you'll likely have to be a lot more proactive. This is normal and shouldn't discourage you.

Don't forget that hosts might receive a ton of messages, so don't take it personally if you don't hear back or they don't invite you. If you don't hear back, follow up. If they don't invite you, move on and apply to another one.

What additional smart tip can you share for other show hosts to consider using?

As I said, high-quality guests are super important to me. That's why I don't rely on the PodMatch algorithm alone when I decide whom to invite. If a potential guest's profile looks like a good fit, I invite them to fill in an application form as a second step. If you'd like to check it out, you can find it here: https://bit.ly/2O2vZPA.

I know a lot of other hosts like to do pre-interviews to assess if a potential guest is a good fit or not, but I prefer to use an application form to keep time in my calendar available for more productive tasks.

Once I'm sure that someone is a good fit, they get to choose if they'd like to do a paid feature or if they prefer to wait until a free interview spot opens up.

I love that having a few paid options allows me to keep my show ad-free and awesome! If you produce a high-quality show, this might be a great way for you to bring in some additional revenue too.

What is your final PodMatch "one thing" you want to leave readers with?

PodMatch is an amazing tool and resource that can save you a ton of time and effort when you're booking new high-quality guests for your show. It's still up to you as the podcast host to define what "high-quality" means for you though. What qualifies someone as a perfect guest for YOUR show might be what disqualifies them for some-one else's show. Make sure you know your show's mission, your ideal listener, your ideal customer, and how your show fits into your entire business concept.

Host: Josh Tapp
https://podmatch.com/member/theluckytitan

So the big question is this: How did some of the world's top entrepreneurs create a cult-like following for their products and services and yet still remain profitable?

I've spent the past 5 years interviewing over 1,000 of the world's most successful entrepreneurs to find out what they did to build their own community of raving fans. On this podcast, we will uncover the secrets that these entrepreneurs used to grow hyperactive social media followings, massive email lists, and paid communities to become the TITANS in their industries.

https://HowtoMonetizeaPodcast.com

CHAPTER 10

THE LUCKY TITAN PODCAST

Why did you join PodMatch as a Podcast Host member?

I still remember when I met Alex Sanfilippo. He was a young guy like me, with a big idea of solving one of the largest problems in our industry: finding VETTED guests for your show. When Alex showed me what he built, I knew I HAD to be part of this incredible community. This platform is a game-changer and should be included in your software stack.

What is one significant way that PodMatch has helped your business/mission?

I use my show not only for content but also for having conversations with my dream clients. PodMatch has such a fantastic vetting tool for guests that it virtually does the work for me. We have generated five sales from PodMatch directly, and then we have generated hundreds of thousands of additional revenue dollars indirectly through the guests with whom we work.

What is your daily routine in PodMatch?

I have my team hop into PodMatch daily with a goal in mind of finding the best of the best. They look through our messages primarily, and then they go through our matches seeking for potential clients to bring on my show. I personally interview these people at least two times per week, which allows for new client conversations multiple times per week.

What do you recommend as the first thing a new Podcast Host member should do after joining PodMatch?

When joining PodMatch, dive into the community. One of the fastest ways to land guesting and hosting deals is through interacting with the community and making REAL connections with other guests and hosts. Having met many of the active members of this community has drastically improved my success as a podcast host and as an entrepreneur.

What do you recommend as the second thing a new Podcast Host member should do after joining PodMatch?

Apply to join the Elite Group! As a member of this group, I can honestly say that this is a GAME-

CHANGING group of amazing people who are seriously moving the podcasting industry forward. I have been on the lookout for a podcast mastermind for years (having started one of my own), but those truly leading the industry are those who join this community.

What "beginner's mistake" did you make with PodMatch that you want to warn other members about?

The biggest mistake most users make when first joining PodMatch is the lack of consistent engagement. I wasn't the exception to that rule. I tried managing this myself, but the truth is, as an entrepreneur, I have multiple inboxes. And if I tried to add an important inbox like PodMatch to my daily list, I would start drowning. Hand the management of this inbox to someone on your team, or hire a virtual assistant to manage this inbox for you on a DAILY basis. Staying consistent with your outreach will keep your show full and your speaking docket at MAX capacity.

What three PodMatch best practices should every Podcast Host use regularly?

1) Respond, respond, respond! Managing your inbox is one of the best ways to keep momentum in your own business and in the business of those you communicate with.

2) Laser focus on your outreach. PodMatch does a fantastic job matching you with potential guests/hosts. But there is an advanced feature filter that is an absolute game-changer for podcast hosts. Simplify your targeting and you won't regret the resulting matches that come from the PodMatch system.

3) Optimize your profile. My host page gets seen hundreds of times each day. Why wouldn't I leverage these views to promote my service. I treat my profile page like a landing page for my company with incredible results.

What smart tip can you share for any Podcast Host to use immediately and benefit from?

Monetize relationships. I've worked with over 1,000 podcast hosts, helping them to monetize their shows, and the common denominator for success among our most profitable shows is the ability to bring TARGETED guests. This doesn't mean these guests need to be "A-listers," but they do need to be your dream clientele. Leveraging the relationships you develop in podcasting will be INVALUABLE in your growth as a podcast host and business owner.

So here's one practice I want you to take out there and apply today:

1) Go to PodMatch. > Do a filtered search. > Find a guest who would be your dream client and invite them on your show.

2) Take some time after your interview (20 minutes or less) to ask your guest these question: *"What is your next big goal? And how can I support you?"*

3) Listen to their response with open ears and an open heart. As you are listening, diagnose what might be holding them back from accomplishing their goals.

4) Recommend a solution. THIS SHOULDN'T BE YOUR OWN SERVICE. First, refer this person to someone who you KNOW can help solve this guest's problem and help them reach their goal.

5) BONUS STEP (for the industry titan): Reach back out to this guest one week later and ask them how their conversation went with your referral, and then give them your BIG ASK.

What additional smart tip can you share for other show hosts to consider using?

I recently worked with a podcast host who had interviewed over 1,000 guests, and he recently joined my Pantheon program to get help with monetizing his podcast. I want this to sink in for you—1,000 interviews—0 sales. What was he doing wrong?! Hundreds of millions of interviews have been completed over the past decade and very few podcasters have EVER tapped into these relationships as potential sales opportunities. So what can you do to make yourself stand out? Be the "Prescribing Physician" for your guests.

Do yourself a favor; on your next interview, I want you to spend 20 minutes following the 4 steps above. Refer your guest to someone else, NOT your own service. After making that referral, I want you to do two things one week later.

1) Reach out to the company you referred your guest to and ask them how the conversation went. Offer to send them more referrals for a small commission.

2) Reach out to the guest you referred and ask them how the conversation went. Then tell them you have a "Big Ask," and then ask for a referral.

I promise you that if you follow these steps, you won't just get a referral, but many of these guests will also ask to be your client. This is a game-changing strategy if you interview guests.

What is your final PodMatch "one thing" you want to leave readers with?

The final thought I want you to consider is a more internal commitment instead of an outward tactic. The term "influencer" or "thought leader" has been bastardized by the rise of social media. So many people have been labeled as leaders who truly aren't what would be considered a "leader of thought" when they simply regurgitate what other "influencers" have said. The saddest part is that many people are doing this without taking time to ask themselves if what they are saying is true.

A few names for you to consider: Galileo, Jesus, Einstein, Mother Theresa, Tony Robbins. *What do all these people have in common?* These were and ARE thought leaders. These individuals took the time to become leaders of thought or "philosophers." The world is STARVING for true leaders of thought, and ANYONE can become a leader of thought if they are willing to become the biggest mover in their industry. Try new things. Test. Fail. THINK! Thought leadership is contrived from time spent observing a problem and inventing solutions.

Be an industry mover. You have a voice. You have an audience. That means you have an obligation to become the best. I can't wait to hear your story!

Host: Doug Thorpe
https://podmatch.com/member/dougthorpe

Doug Thorpe is a performance-driven senior executive, entrepreneur, board member, thought leader, and consultant with more than 40 years of success in the financial services, executive coaching, oil & gas, and healthcare industries. Leveraging extensive experience in guiding business transformation for growth-oriented organizations, he is a trusted guide for mid-cap companies to large global enterprises requiring expert assistance with leadership development, team performance, employee engagement, culture shifts, and change management. Visit:

https://DougThorpe.com

https://Podcasts.DougThorpe.com

CHAPTER 11

LEADERSHIP POWERED BY COMMON SENSE

Why did you join PodMatch as a Podcast Host member?

I had been dabbling with podcasting since 2009. Recording some shows was a way to share information from my old non-profit network. However, as my executive coaching and business advisory practice took off in 2015, I knew that podcasting would one day be a key strategy for me. I had tried various other platforms to recruit guests for the show but was never especially happy with the level of expertise in those groups. Then I found PodMatch. Immediately, I discovered high-quality, motivated guests for my show. People had great stories and ideas to share with my audience. I was hooked. That was Q4, 2021.

Since then, I've produced almost 100 shows and have loved every minute of it. Reviews are pouring in. I started publishing only one show a week, then ramped to two. Soon I will be releasing three shows every week. I'm seeing over 500 downloads per week, which gets me into the Apple iTunes top 10%. I couldn't be happier about those results.

And actual revenue dollars have started coming in. So doing all the steps you will learn from PodMatch can make a big difference for you.

What is one significant way that PodMatch has helped your business/mission?

It is very important to me to have good guests and meaningful discussions on my show. I don't do puff pieces with foolish ideas. Not that good fun entertainment is bad. I just am not about that for my audience. I serve business leaders who are already successful and looking for bonus material to give them an edge. You don't get that in puff pieces. Rather, I want thought-provoking ideas, answers, and motivations to help my audience thrive.

I know there are thousands of coaches trying to help people with many different things. I am establishing my brand using the trademark "Leadership Powered by Common Sense." It has resonated well with my audience. Using Pod-Match has helped me find professionals, authors, and specialists who can speak the same specialty language of business that I speak thus allowing a bigger, broader discussion to benefit my audience.

What is your daily routine in PodMatch?

I check the dashboard daily. The message queue is important to me. Once I check for possible new matches, I browse that list and send invitations to sit for prep calls. I insist my guests do a prep call with me. I want to meet, see, and know my guests even before the invitation to record goes out. Fortunately, with PodMatch, I seldom have to reject someone after the prep call.

What do you recommend as the first thing a new Podcast Host member should do after joining PodMatch?

I recommend you take the training, then do it again. There truly is a lot to grasp, but all of it is important to get the best benefit from Alex's great platform. Get a functional appreciation for how everything fits together. Follow the flow. Don't get ahead of yourself. The flow makes sense once you learn it.

After you master the basics, run wild with it! Get creative. Explore every aspect. And if you get stuck somewhere, send in a support request. The PodMatch team is awesome.

What do you recommend as the second thing a new Podcast Host member should do after joining PodMatch?

Decide on your perfect guest profile, then be intentional in looking at matches. Ask questions and explore. This place is a gold mine. You won't be disappointed.

What "beginner's mistake" did you make with PodMatch that you want to warn other members about?

I didn't have my own system for setting up and producing a show. My first few dozen invitations got scrambled on my end. I was booking appointments via Calendly® (my other tool) but wasn't thinking about the volume. I created a Google sheet for myself to track my invitations, prep call dates, and eventually all aspects of each episode/guest I booked.

I now track everything from the first invitation to chat via the prep call all the way through final production and release. That may sound like a problem, but it's not with a simple Google sheet to track things. That way, I can have guests at various stages in my work queue and know exactly where they are with everything I want to do on my shows.

What three PodMatch best practices should every Podcast Host use regularly?

First, check the matches the system gives you. Respond quickly. Then be intentional. You want to build a brand with your podcast. Hopping from guest to guest and topic to topic can confuse the brand. Don't do that.

Instead, decide on a range of topics, ideas, and guests that can serve your brand. Book those people first. If you run across an occasional guest that seems way off the mainstream but is interesting to you, they might be good for your audience too. Talk to them and decide whether there is an angle to explore that can add value to your brand even if it is "out there" somewhere.

Next, use the PodMatch dashboard regularly. Keep up with dates, times, and people that way. Check show status for each guest against your own system of tracking (see above).

Lastly, be responsive. If someone messages you, let them get a reply from you as quickly as possible. I know I said it before, but that is a big part of keeping this network alive.

What smart tip can you share for any Podcast Host to use immediately and benefit from?

Be yourself. Don't copy someone else's style, voice, mannerisms, or punch lines. Find your true self. That comes through on podcasts. Be authentic; get real. If you curse, let it flow naturally. Don't act like a choirboy on your show, then show up with guns blazing for a client. And vice versa.

Just be real.

Remember, the person you may want to copy already exists. The world doesn't need another one of them. It needs you. You were put here for a reason. Celebrate that. Let your passion for the topic area you want to explore shine through!

I promise you'll find your niche audience.

What additional smart tip can you share for other show hosts to consider using?

When you are first starting out, it will feel overwhelming. Take things a day at a time, step by step. Enjoy the experience; don't let it create a big burden on you. Think about the one person in your audience you will be helping with your message. Do it for them, not yourself.

Then the next day, think about another person you will be helping, then another, another, and so on. Pretty soon you will feel the momentum building. Building a show brand is like a giant flywheel. It takes great amounts of energy to get it moving. Yet once it is in motion, it maintains that momentum by itself.

What is your final PodMatch "one thing" you want to leave readers with?

The success of your show depends on many things. However, I believe two things matter most. After you get all your basic tech stuff resolved, you need to think about how you want to conduct the show and interviews. Then you must have quality guest spots to help make the show pop. You might be a fabulous host, but if your guest is flatlined or has no personality whatsoever, your show will flop.

Using the tools and network in PodMatch helps elevate the guest piece significantly. I prefer to conduct a host interview "prep" time. I make my prospective guests attend a 15-minute interview about being interviewed. If they don't connect well, have chemistry with me, or I feel their subject matter doesn't fit, I'd rather know that sooner than later. If that sounds like some kind of podcast snobbery, I'm sorry. I think it is a must. And yes, I have turned down potential guests who say they are too busy to do that.

My show is a big part of my brand. My guests need to serve the audience I serve. We must be able to have a fun, spirited discussion about the topics. I believe if that isn't happening, I'm wasting time all around. The world doesn't need more noise, but it does need valuable insights, inspiration, and help.

Host: Tim Heale
https://podmatch.com/member/timheale

Did you ever wish to know more about the lives of your ancestors? I traced my family tree only to find there was limited information available. I discovered a photograph of my great-grandfather and wanted to know more about him, what he had experienced during his lifetime and build up a meaningful picture of what life was like back then. I never got to speak with past members of my family or have stories handed down through the generations. So I started a fascinating series recording ordinary people's life stories who want to leave legacies for future generations to enjoy and learn from. Through PodMatch, I have met some awesome people whose adventures and extraordinary tales can now be shared and enjoyed forevermore.

https://buzzsprout.com/1118723

CHAPTER 12

ORDINARY PEOPLE'S EXTRAORDINARY STORIES

Why did you join PodMatch as a Podcast Host member?

I had exhausted my immediate network of friends and family who wanted to tell their life stories and was scratching around to find people who wanted to come on my podcasts. I saw an advertisement on Buzzsprout detailing how to find guests. This prompted me to join PodMatch, and I have never looked back.

PodMatch has given me an inexhaustible source of guests for my own show. It has also enabled me to be matched with other podcasters as a guest on their shows. This has given me the opportunity to broaden my own audience and meet with a wider variety of people from all walks of life which I would not have otherwise had access to.

PodMatch is so easy to use and very intuitive. It takes out all the hard work in finding not only guests but also hosts.

What is one significant way that PodMatch has helped your business/mission?

I feel I have a mission to get as many ordinary people as possible to tell their extraordinary life stories. This will enable future generations to gain first-hand insight into our current period of time. It is amazing what people have experienced and achieved during their lifetime. My podcast guests may not all be well known celebrities, but they each have fascinating stories to share.

PodMatch has been instrumental in finding many people who are willing to talk on my podcast and to also be on camera. It has been an awesome experience.

What is your daily routine in PodMatch?

I generally check a couple of times a day to see if I have any matches, then I reply to messages from anyone that would like to come on my show. I then go to the explore button and look for people who I would like to interview and invite onto the show. The great thing about scheduling through PodMatch is it will automatically work out time zone differences. For example, if you are in BST and your guest is in EST, PodMatch will show both local times and do the calculations for you.

What do you recommend as the first thing a new Podcast Host member should do after joining PodMatch?

I recommend having a clear idea of the type of guest you are looking for before setting up your ideal guest profile and podcast page. Then look at the notes for each section before populating that section. I recommend looking carefully at the guest criteria, keywords and tags for your perfect guests. The notes will help you abide by best practices. Check through these sections and make sure you are happy with everything you put in place before confirming and going live.

What do you recommend as the second thing a new Podcast Host member should do after joining PodMatch?

Pace yourself. Have a clear idea of your ideal guest, and send them a request. If you already have matches, only send a few requests at a time, as it is very easy to get carried away and get overwhelmed by responses. To assist with possible overloads, PodMatch limits the number of matches per day. I suggest using an application such as Calendly® to manage your guest requests and make sure you copy each scheduled interview into PodMatch. By doing this, you won't miss a guest schedule.

What "beginner's mistake" did you make with PodMatch that you want to warn other members about?

My enthusiasm ran away with me at first, and I needed to reign myself in. I made the mistake of trying to book too many guest interviews within a tight timeframe. I found many people responded positively to me but wanted to come on my show on the same day that they had messaged me. I quickly learned the art of patience and now only invite a couple of guests at any one time. I give them a few days to confirm or pass before inviting more guests. Take your time, and look at the longer picture. Don't get too hung up on "clocking up" guest numbers. It will take time to build your audience, so don't be disappointed if you begin with only a few downloads when you had anticipated becoming an overnight star with thousands of followers! Don't give up at the first hurdle. Enjoy it, and keep trying to improve your technique.

What three PodMatch best practices should every Podcast Host use regularly?

1) Be selective when looking for the right guest for your show. Vet guest profiles carefully, and don't in haste invite a guest onto your show with the wrong criteria.

2) Concentrate on the quality of your content, questions, audio and visual for your podcast, and strive to become the best you can whilst maintaining your own personality.

3) Don't try to do too much too soon. Allow yourself plenty of time to edit and upload your content. Try to do this on a regular day and time, as consistency works for the listeners/viewers.

What smart tip can you share for any Podcast Host to use immediately and benefit from?

Have a very clear idea of what your goals are, what your podcast is about and who your target audience is. Have a plan, and pace yourself. Practice the art of hosting. Remember you have two ears and one mouth, and use them in that ratio. Think about how to frame your questions to encourage conversations to flow, rather than using closed questions where yes or no answers may follow. Don't speak over your guest; give them time to answer the questions. Speak clearly, and try not to say "um." Do your homework, and investigate other show formats of similar content to yours. Compare how other hosts conduct their interviews. This will improve your own style and help you gain confidence to explore new techniques. Be yourself as no one wants to listen to a carbon copy of someone else's show.

What additional smart tip can you share for other show hosts to consider using?

Think about how you will record your show, in person or remotely. What platform will you use (StreamYard, Ecamm, Riverside.fm, Zoom, etc.)? Invest time and effort in researching which platforms work for you.

What equipment do you need (iPhone, laptop, interface, microphones, mixing desk, camera etc.)?

Set yourself a budget for equipment.

What editing software will you use (Adobe Audition, Audacity®, GarageBand, Premier Pro, Final Cut Pro, etc.)?

How much time can you realistically dedicate to each episode? Don't forget to factor in other commitments, such as family and work schedules. Remember time zones may affect your own sleeping patterns.

How long will each episode be (5 minutes, 2 hours, anything in-between)? Allow editing time.

When will you publish each episode (once a week, bi-weekly, once a month)?

What are your hosting plans (e.g., Anchor® is free; Buzzsprout and YouTube have paid plans, etc.)?

What is your final PodMatch "one thing" you want to leave readers with?

Be very clear why you want to be a podcast creator, and remind yourself regularly why you are doing it. If it is no longer enjoyable, it is time to move on. It can be disheartening in the early days when you can't see your audience growing quickly enough for your expectations. Have patience. It may take some time to grow. After all, *"Rome wasn't built in a day."*

Host: Walter Crosby

https://podmatch.com/member/salesandcigars

How do you increase sales in your organization? Host Walter Crosby sits down with cigar in hand and has growth-minded conversations proven to boost sales. Crosby sets the table by identifying areas where you can excel by first acknowledging the misunderstandings. Like every great sales person, he takes time to reflect, strategize and execute. Sit back, listen in, and puff that cigar because Walter Crosby will light you up!

http://SalesandCigars.com

CHAPTER 13

SALES & CIGARS PODCAST

Why did you join PodMatch as a Podcast Host member?

I started a podcast in May of 2020 for two reasons. I wanted to help entrepreneurs and sales professionals think differently about sales. To me, sales is a wonderful profession, but most people in sales see it as a job. The other reason was a platform to discuss cigars. Every guest is asked if they have a relationship with cigars. Usually, there is an interesting story or a great memory that comes out.

I joined PodMatch because after scheduling 45 guests just from my network, I started to feel pressure to find new guests. My assistant did some research on options for hosts to connect with viable guests. We quickly landed on Pod-Match because the platform was well-supported and rich with guest options.

What is one significant way that PodMatch has helped your business/mission?

My podcast is focused around finding guests who have a point of view on sales and can add value to my audience with ideas, best practices, or just different perspectives. PodMatch allows me to ensure a good match for the type of conversation I want to have. To accomplish my goal, I need smart, passionate guests with a perspective. PodMatch attracts a high-quality guest and allows me to determine if they are a good fit before investing the time into an interview. With a weekly podcast, I need to deliver each and every week—PodMatch makes that possible.

What is your daily routine in PodMatch?

I am in PodMatch twice a day. Once, I am looking for guests, reviewing matches and requests, and also actively looking for guests and making invites. The second time, I am looking for opportunities to be a guest on other podcasts that are a good fit. I spend about 10 minutes in the morning and 10 minutes in the evening. The trick is being consistent.

What do you recommend as the first thing a new Podcast Host member should do after joining PodMatch?

Watch the educational videos that are available. You may want to watch them more than once. The videos will shorten your learning curve, and you get traction with the platform so much faster.

What do you recommend as the second thing a new Podcast Host member should do after joining PodMatch?

Build out a strong Podcast Page. The more robust the better. Provide as much of the information as you have, and go back and update your page quarterly. You are constantly adding to your podcast; don't forget to update the Podcast Page. The more accurate your data, the more accurate PodMatch can be with the ability to line up guests.

This is the best way to help guests and other hosts know what your show is about and why they might consider being a guest.

What "beginner's mistake" did you make with PodMatch that you want to warn other members about?

Oscar Wilde said, "*Experience is the name I give to my mistakes.*" Well, I have a lot of experience, and my start with PodMatch was no different. The biggest mistake I made was not engaging with PodMatch every day. PodMatch can automatically deliver matches, but as a Host or a Guest, you have to engage consistently. Look at it this way, you are going to get out of it what you put into it. Don't sit on the sidelines.

What three PodMatch best practices should every Podcast Host use regularly?

1) Be clear about what your podcast is about.

2) Use PodMatch at least once a day.

3) Be generous with your reviews of others.

What smart tip can you share for any Podcast Host to use immediately and benefit from?

You want to look like a professional Podcast Host. Make sure you add quality guests that fit your program, and make it easy for the guest to schedule once you have decided to have them as a guest. We always send a little gift to our guests as a thank you.

What additional smart tip can you share for other show hosts to consider using?

Once you work through your network of people, finding guests can be a challenge. PodMatch can help you keep a steady stream of quality guests to be on your podcast. You have invested the time and resources to build a podcast. Engage with PodMatch consistently to build your awareness.

What is your final PodMatch "one thing" you want to leave readers with?

You are going to get out of PodMatch what you put into it. The platform was built for you. Use it consistently; 15 minutes in the morning and 15 minutes in the evening is enough to get great value. Be a great host.

Host: Peter George
https://podmatch.com/member/petergeorge

D o you want to be a better speaker? Do you want to know how to craft and deliver a talk that connects with people on all levels? Do you want to be calm, confident, and credible every time you speak? Then tune in to "Public Speaking with Peter George." It's the only public speaking show that has two helpful episodes per week: one with a guest expert who shares with you tips, techniques, and ideas; and one QuickBites episode where Peter gives a specific tip in five minutes or less. Each of these is designed to help you develop superior public speaking skills so you can increase your impact, influence, and income whether you're speaking on stage, presenting in meetings, or selling to prospects.

https://PeterGeorgePublicSpeaking.com

CHAPTER 14

PUBLIC SPEAKING WITH PETER GEORGE

Why did you join PodMatch as a Podcast Host member?

When first planning my podcast, "Public Speaking with Peter George," I thought about many things, such as equipment, studio setup, sound quality, editing, building an audience, and guests. Okay, that last one is not entirely true. I believed getting guests would be reasonably easy. After all, guests want exposure. All I'd have to do was send an email, and we'd set up a date for the recording. Likewise, potential guests would contact me, asking to be on my show. Well, I misjudged. Actually, I was flat-out wrong.

I had several big names lined up at the beginning, which was great! But I neglected to consider the amount of time it took to get those first six or seven guests. Once I contacted them, we had to work the interview into our busy schedules.

Another thing I didn't consider was that once you start recording, editing, and writing show notes every week, prospecting—which was once fun—becomes a chore.

It was just about this time that I learned about PodMatch. It was a relatively new service that solved my problems and frustrations.

What is one significant way that PodMatch has helped your business/mission?

Podcasting, in general, has had a remarkable impact on my business. For instance, my book, *The Captivating Public Speaker: Engage, Impact, and Inspire Your Audience Every Time*, has 14 endorsements in the front. And 11 of the experts who provided these endorsements were guests on my show. And I connected with all but one of them through PodMatch. Likewise, there are subject authorities who I met through PodMatch cited in my book. I couldn't be more grateful to the founder of PodMatch, Alex Sanfilippo (one of those who wrote an endorsement), and his team for their effect on my business.

What is your daily routine in PodMatch?

As a host, I use PodMatch weekly, which fits into my routine and serves me well. During this time, I follow a fairly consistent process.

1) Review the dashboard. This helps ensure that the guests and I get the most from the system and experience.

2) Answer inquiries from those who would like to be on my show.

3) Follow up with guests who have just recorded interviews with me.

4) Explore for guests who I might want to feature on my show.

I can't imagine how long all this would take without the PodMatch system. But because the system is easy to navigate, my time there is spent efficiently and effectively.

What do you recommend as the first thing a new Podcast Host member should do after joining PodMatch?

Without a doubt, the first thing you should do is watch the educational videos. To be honest, I didn't watch them at first. Instead, I checked things out on my own—clicking on this button and that link, seeing what each one did. Then I learned that you get credit towards your ranking on the leaderboard when you complete the videos. Being competitive, I had to watch the videos. So, I played them but without really paying attention.

Then one day, while on indefinite hold with a service provider, I truly listened to one of the videos and found the information more than helpful. Immediately, I went back and watched the others. When I was done, I wished I had watched them sooner. The short time it takes to view them delivers a return on your investment many times over.

What do you recommend as the second thing a new Podcast Host member should do after joining PodMatch?

I suggest you put time into your podcast profile page. It's here that guests will determine if they want to be on your show.

When you are completing this profile, be specific! The more specific you are, the more likely the right guests will contact you. Ultimately, this makes the experience for you and your potential guests more effective. It also helps you attract guests who will benefit your listeners.

If completing your show's profile sounds daunting, don't worry. Each section guides you along. I suggest you also look at the pages of successful hosts and emulate them. Although you want this page to be helpful to you and your potential guests, please do not overthink this initially. You can always go back and edit it.

What "beginner's mistake" did you make with PodMatch that you want to warn other members about?

Aside from not watching the educational videos right away, another mistake I made was not setting specific expectations—for myself or my guests. As a result, potential guests started contacting me. Most were people who would benefit my audience. But because I wasn't as specific as I should have been, many people were not the right fit. I soon realized I needed to determine who would make a good guest and who would not.

You might think that this would bring inquiries to a trickle. It did not. In fact, more people contacted me, asking to be on my show. The best part was that the vast majority of them were a great fit. This increased the quality of information and value I could provide to my listeners.

Another expectation you want to set is the quality of your show's audio. Listeners will quickly turn off a show with poor audio. So be sure to help your guests understand the importance of good audio on their end. In my opinion, this includes using an external mic instead of their computer's mic and being in a quiet room that is free of distractions and noise.

Because I didn't set this expectation early enough, I recorded some shows where the information was great, but the audio on the guests' end was terrible. Consequently, I did not use these recordings.

What three PodMatch best practices should every Podcast Host use regularly?

The three practices every PodMatch host should be concerned with are: #1 consistency, #2 consistency, and #3 consistency. The more helpful response is to respect your guests. Respecting your guests includes making things clear and straightforward for them, including expectations, the length of the interview, whether the recording is audio only or also video, and other information that might be helpful.

The ultimate sign of respect is to show up! You would not think this has to be said, but it does. Short of an emergency, show up! Your guests put aside time for your show and spend time on preparation. It matters.

What smart tip can you share for any Podcast Host to use immediately and benefit from?

Alex Sanfilippo and his team created PodMatch to be a matchmaking service for guests and hosts, and it does a superb job at this. But its functionality goes even deeper. PodMatch is a matchmaking service for guests and your listeners.

Always ask yourself: *"Is this potential guest someone who aligns with my show, values, and listeners' wants and needs?* If yes, great. If not, move on.

What additional smart tip can you share for other show hosts to consider using?

Ask your guest to provide questions pertaining to the topic you will discuss. I ask for seven to ten. Having these questions is not meant to replace your preparation. Instead, it helps ensure your guests give prior thought to the interview. It also helps by providing you with go-to questions should the interview get bogged down.

Another thing you might want to do is ask your guest to explain how your discussion will benefit your audience. Their answer serves as a model for your show's introduction and the show notes that inform your listeners how they will benefit from listening to that particular episode.

What is your final PodMatch "one thing" you want to leave readers with?

Alex and the team at PodMatch have created a superb platform that helps you produce shows that serve your listeners. However, the key to this platform is you. Put the time and effort into it, and you will prosper.

Host: Vicki Noethling
https://podmatch.com/member/vickinoethling

The Find Your Leadership Confidence Podcast brings new voices and new perspectives into the conversation. You will discover and enjoy innovative insights that move you forward.

Whether you're an introvert, extrovert, or anything in between, find yourself getting inspired and enjoy the journey of emerging as a leader of exception in the 21st century!

Our audience is women entrepreneurs and small business owners who are looking to improve how they present themselves to their audience and to grow and enhance their skills as leaders who are ready to show the world the greatness that they have inside.

https://FindYourLeadershipConfidence.com

CHAPTER #15

THE FIND YOUR LEADERSHIP CONFIDENCE PODCAST

Why did you join PodMatch as a Podcast Host member?

I had just started my podcast in March of 2022. At first, I expected I would do four podcasts a month. Then I had gotten a good list of potential guests from two joint venture sessions that I attended, but those lists did not include things like bio, topics, questions, social media links, etc. That meant I had to do all that research if the guest did not have a One Sheet. That was time I really did not have to spend. This is also important because when I post the episode, I have a system in place that easily can pull in the information from PodMatch and/or my application. That makes the time it takes me to post the episode cut in half.

I joined PodMatch as a Podcast Host member to be able to reach more potential guests that fit my target audience. The system that was put in place makes the process very smooth and easy to manage. Almost everything is there. My application is quite similar, so if they don't fill that out, I know I can just go to their profile page and cut and paste what I need to prepare for the interview. Again, the ease of use of the system makes this a no-brainer. I also loved the idea of getting paid for hosting!

What is one significant way that PodMatch has helped your business/mission?

It is hard to believe that I have recorded over 66 interviews in just a few months, and it is due to the continual influx of great guests that are matched to me each day. I have been so impressed with the caliber of podcast guests on this platform and continue to recommend it to my fellow speakers and coaches who are thinking about doing a podcast of their own. My mission is to provide my target audience the resources and connections that will help them grow their businesses, and PodMatch is making that come true. One of my goals was to have a variety of guests/topics that I could group on my website to be more helpful for my visitors. With the number of interviews I now am conducting, I will reach that goal before the 4th quarter. Thank you PodMatch!

What is your daily routine in PodMatch?

I usually go to my Dashboard mid-morning and early evening. Most of my podcasts are done after 4:00 pm and wrap up by 9:30 or 10:00 pm. I use the morning sessions, which usually are about 30 minutes to 1 hour, to respond to other's messages and to find matches. The evening sessions are to do final preparation work and messaging to my guests. I use this time to send my follow-up emails to request that my application be completed and scheduling of the interview. Once we get close to the date, I send an email to help them prepare for the interview, sharing the title of the episode and the questions I will ask them. Post interview, I use this time to be sure I captured their photos and social media information to use in my posting to YouTube and my website.

What do you recommend as the first thing a new Podcast Host member should do after joining PodMatch?

Fill out your profile as clearly and concisely as possible so you get a good match. And add those photos! The most gratifying thing is to have a potential match and read through their information and think, "*Wow, you will make a great guest!*" When I first joined, I just put one photo out there, but I noticed others had a few choices to pick from, and I liked that. I am now adding more photos to my profile as well.

What do you recommend as the second thing a new Podcast Host member should do after joining PodMatch?

Start reviewing your potential matches. While some of the matches are at the 64%–65% range, which is my target starting point, I still read through their information to be sure it is a good fit. Sometimes you might find a few are the same topic in a row, and I mark them to visit later. Some are more corporate driven, and I pass on those because my audience is more entrepreneur centric. I also take advantage of listening to some of their video clips or links to podcasts they have been on to get a feel for them as a guest. For me, it is being prepared but still making the interview feel like a conversation with a couple of friends.

What "beginner's mistake" did you make with PodMatch that you want to warn other members about?

I did not block out times on my scheduling calendar where I had other meetings that are on my other work/personal calendars or times I simply did not want to do a podcast due to vacation or family gathering. That led to some schedule changes. Lesson Learned.

What three PodMatch best practices should every Podcast Host use regularly?

1) Be prepared and do your follow-up. I think the guest appreciates that you took the time to be prepared, and it makes the interview flow well.

2) Show up—smiling and ready to bring the energy. There is nothing worse than you getting on that Zoom and no one joins. I am guilty of this myself and have put in multiple notifications to avoid it happening. The smile and energy are just contagious and again make the interview so much better.

3) Enjoy the time you have with your guest. I want the guest to feel like the time flew by and look forward to another time where we can join for another great conversation. I feel that if the two of us feel that way, it will surely extend out to our audience.

What smart tip can you share for any Podcast Host to use immediately and benefit from?

Send several messages to keep engaged with your guest with the goal of making them feel comfortable from the start. I want to be there to answer their questions, make changes if necessary and be sure they know that I will be there on time and ready to roll!

What additional smart tip can you share for other show hosts to consider using?

I do a lighting and sound checks and review of my slide with their info before we start recording just to do one final check.

What is your final PodMatch "one thing" you want to leave readers with?

PodMatch is a wonderful resource for podcasters and guests. It is that connection that was missing. It is a quick, efficient, and effective tool to find that perfect guest who will be able to impact your audience with the gifts that they bring to the table. I am so grateful for what they are doing as this constant influx of guests is making me a better host, and we all win when that happens. I hope, too, that this will encourage others to venture out there and become a member of Pod-Match so we can continue to get these wonderful guests to interview.

The "Find Your Leadership Confidence Podcast"
Profile Page on PodMatch

Host: Nickolas Natali
https://podmatch.com/member/nickolasnatali

The Nickolas Natali Show is a podcast where experts, entrepreneurs and entertainers are interviewed and bring new perspectives on how to live a more fulfilling life and take your business to the next level.

The show is a blend of research-based interviews, and more often than not, it's a couple of kooky birds choppin' it up. People are saying "The Nickolas Natali Show" is soon to outpace "The Joe Rogan Show," "The Tim Ferriss Show," and the likes! By "people," we mean Nick's mother.

https://NickolasNatali.com

THE NICKOLAS NATALI SHOW

Why did you join PodMatch as a Podcast Host member?

I wish I could sugarcoat this story, but I can't. I lived in a 1986 Chevy Suburban to pay off my student loans. I had roughly $60,000 in debt and worked 60- to 80-hour weeks to pay it off as quickly as possible. I aimed to keep my expenses as low as possible and ended up suffering from malnutrition because of it. While traveling from parking lot to parking lot, from sketchy streets to abandoned cul-de-sacs, I met some of the most incredible people. For reasons unknown, the 'burb brought people together and gave them a safe place to tell their life stories.

After I paid off my debt, I wanted to continue to meet people who had done amazing things, lived adventurously, and found ways to make their life fulfilling. This led me to start a podcast and ultimately join PodMatch as a host member. After moving out of the 'burb, PodMatch has become the much-needed safe haven to meet high-quality podcast guests, each with their own set of unique experiences and outlooks that can make any podcast rich with wisdom.

What is one significant way that PodMatch has helped your business/mission?

There's an area in Southern California that is nicknamed the "Dirty D." I grew up in that area. As a kid, the Dirty D wasn't crawling with creatives, entrepreneurs, and experts. The tendency I had of thinking outside of the box didn't get me into huge trouble, but I was sent to the principal a few times for selling candy bars out of my backpack in middle school.

PodMatch has made me realize that I'm not the only one that's always had the "itch." Not the kind that you have to go see a doctor for but the kind that makes you jump out of bed to do amazing things. Think differently. Dream bigger. Take risks. Love without fear. Despite what scientists are saying, I like to think that people are at the center of our world. Being in community with one another gives *so* much meaning to our lives, and having a place to connect with people that have done greater things than I have has empowered me to grow professionally and personally.

What is your daily routine in PodMatch?

Wake up. Ignore the celebrities in my DMs. Log in to PodMatch. Connect with guests that can bring the house down, and lock them on the calendar.

What do you recommend as the first thing a new Podcast Host member should do after joining PodMatch?

If you are new to PodMatch, welcome! The first thing I would do as a PodMatch host is understand who your *ideal* guest would be. What are they knowledgeable in? Are they funny? Do they need to have a certain number of years in your industry? There are so many outstanding guests to choose from on PodMatch that the difficulty arises in narrowing them down to have the best fit for *your* podcast.

The expert in scuba diving is probably a rock star guest but may not serve your audience best if you're the host of the "How Plants Grow" podcast. The first step I would recommend would be to build a system to qualify your guests before bringing them on your show. (Google Forms, TypeForm™, etc., will do!) That way, your heart doesn't get in the way of your head, and you know you're providing a consistent and reliable experience for your specific audience.

What do you recommend as the second thing a new Podcast Host member should do after joining PodMatch?

Don't let your guests turn into strangers. Through PodMatch, I've made friends that I intend on keeping for the rest of my days! It's easy to have a guest show up, you both clock in for an hour, then part ways to never speak to each other again. Don't let this happen. Keep in touch because at the end of the day, as much as this is about growing your business and expanding your network, if you're not making friends along the way, you are doing it **wrong**.

What "beginner's mistake" did you make with PodMatch that you want to warn other members about?

Rejection, along with spiders, continues to climb year after year as one of the top fears people go toe to toe with. Entrepreneurship, creative endeavors—and anything worth pursuing—comes with a side dish of rejection. PodMatch is no exception, and it is not personal. There will be fantastic guests with raving reviews that will turn down your invitation to join you on your podcast. That doesn't mean your podcast stinks; they don't think you're smelly. As you learn to wean out guests that may not be the right fit for your show, you'll find that guests are going to do the same with podcasts they are willing to join. Don't take it personally! Brush it off, get back out there, and as Zac Efron said in *High School Musical*, *"Get'cha head in the game!"*

What three PodMatch best practices should every Podcast Host use regularly?

1) Don't mass blast or generalize messages. It may take more time, but the personal touch is always appreciated.

2) Don't seek to sell; seek to serve.

3) Fill out that profile in detail! It's hard to connect with people we don't have enough information about!

What smart tip can you share for any Podcast Host to use immediately and benefit from?

It must be said: Podcast hosts are simply not doing enough research on their guests. They're not. If you want to stand out, bring the best out of your guests, and serve your audience the way they deserve, then do your research. It makes all the difference, and your audience will thank you for it.

What additional smart tip can you share for other show hosts to consider using?

Ever heard of a two-for-one combo? It may not be what you ordered, but it's what you're going to get. The first smart tip I have for you is to know that the only way you lose is if you quit. Podcasting is a long-term play. Staying consistent in podcasting innately breeds higher quality and growth over time. Most podcasts grow via word of mouth, and it is crucial you provide your audience with consistency and give them your best, week in and week out.

The second smart tip in this combo meal is to treat your guests like royalty. I'm not saying bend to their every need and demand, but I am saying make them feel valued, treat them with respect, and show a genuine interest in the topics you are covering. A guest that comes on your show is taking the risk that you will value their time as you value your own. As much as the quality of the episode relies on you, it also relies on them! You'd be surprised how far a smile and a compliment out of the gate can go.

What is your final PodMatch "one thing" you want to leave readers with?

The beautiful and oddly terrifying thing about podcasting is that there is nowhere to hide! Wherever you go, there you are. My encouragement to you would be to own your story and where you are at. As with anything public facing, there is a tendency to accidentally sign up for the comparison game. As you'll soon find, there are *many* accomplished individuals here on Pod-Match!

Don't look at the top host/shows/guest list with envy or jealousy, but instead, celebrate others' accomplishments! There is nothing to gain from coveting except internal turmoil. Podcasts are intended to be a shared experience to connect with one another, amplify servitude, and push progress forward for every party involved—host, guest, and listener! Go all in, focus on owning *your* story, and everything will fall into place.

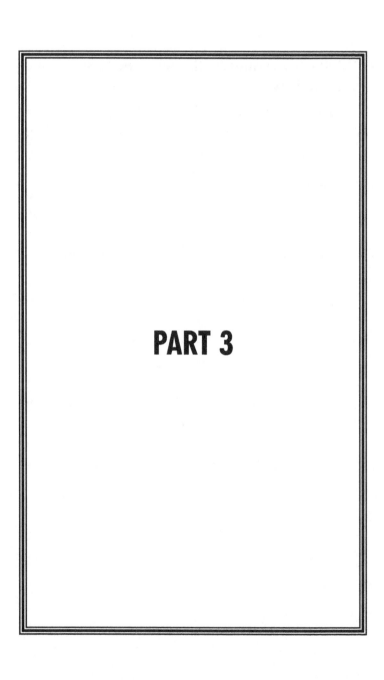

PART 3

BONUS RESOURCES

GIFTS FOR READERS

To further increase the value and impact of this book, we asked members to offer a valuable gift for readers to help them with their podcast hosting journey. We hope you enjoy and profit from these gifts.

Mike Capuzzi's gift:

I help business owners, entrepreneurs and corporate leaders write and publish short, helpful books that are quick to read and easy to publish. I am offering readers of PodMatch Host Mastery the opportunity to get my *Short Book Magic Kit*, which includes three valuable books, including my Amazon #1 best selling book, *The Magic of Short Books.* Visit:

https://MikeCapuzzi.com/podmatch-books

Tonya Eberhart & Michael Carr's gift:

Want to know how to attract more, convert more, and charge more for your services while spending less on marketing? Download our FREE guide and learn how to build an outstanding personal brand:

https://BrandFaceforExperts.com/guide

Beate Chelette's gift:

What's your #1 Business Growth Blocker quiz? Take the free 2 minute quiz to find out what your #1 Business Growth Blocker is and get a report that tells you what the secrets are to growing your business consistently and how to remove your Business Growth Blocker immediately. Visit:

http://GrowthBlockerQuiz.com

Jonathan McLernon's gift:

For (aspiring) online coaches, I wrote an e-book called *The 28-Day Coach* that teaches you how to build and launch an online coaching business within 28 days. You can sign up to grab a copy at this link here:

https://JonMcLernon.link/28-day-coach

Wade Galt's gift:

Screen guests to attract givers (and possible promotional partners). Get Wade's suggested PodMatch guest screening checklist & scoring system for you and your team. Visit:

https://www.3DayWeekendEntrepreneur.com/ podmatch-host-book

Claudia Garbutt's gift:

The Instant Podcast Monetization Guide is for high-ticket coaches and other service-based entrepreneurs who want to launch their own Top 10 podcast as their personal authority marketing machine that helps them go from "best-kept secret" to "go-to expert" and that they can monetize straight from the start (without ads or having to grow a large audience first).

https://WiredforSuccess.solutions/podcasting-for -business-growth

Josh Tapp's gift:

The Pantheon Method is a FREE mini course that covers our 7-phase podcast monetization system. We use this system to constantly close 5-, 6- and even 7-figure deals from our podcast every single day.

https://HowtoMonetizeaPodcast.com

Doug Thorpe's gift:

I'm offering a free copy of my latest book *Trust at Work*. Visit:

https://DougThorpe.com/bookdeal

Walter Crosby's gift:

I have a FREE BOOK for growth-minded entrepreneurs who are frustrated with not understanding why their revenue forecast is always wrong and unreliable. It's called *7 Big Mistakes CEOs Make with Their Revenue Forecast*. They just need to email walter@helixsalesdevelopment.com and reference this book.

Peter George's gift:

Do you want to be calm, confident, and credible® every time you speak? Then get your Free Weekly Public Speaking Tips at:

https://PeterGeorgePublicSpeaking.com/tips

Victoria Noethling's gift:

Want to make a bigger impact on your next podcast? Then you will want to get Vicki's *5 On-Camera Essentials*. This is a handy checklist for you to keep by your computer to ensure you're putting your best face forward!

Email vicki.noethling@gmail.com for your copy.

Nickolas Natali's gift:

There are many one-off resources for starting a podcast, however, there are not many on how to sustain a podcast! Most podcasts stop after just seven episodes, don't let this be you. You can find a free 15-minute training about everything you need to know for longevity in podcasting here:

https://Youtube.com/NickolasNatali

NOT A PODMATCH
MEMBER YET?

PodMatch is the premier site for podcast hosts to find interesting and powerful guests.

With two value-packed membership levels, joining PodMatch is one of the smartest and most cost-effective ways to find quality guests for your show.

Joining the PodMatch family is quick and simple. Just visit:

https://podmatch.com/signup/today

Made in the USA
Monee, IL
25 April 2023

32491109R00085